The Developing Child

Recent decades have witnessed unprecedented advances in research on human development. In those same decades there have been profound changes in public policy toward children. Each book in the Developing Child series reflects the importance of such research in its own right and as it bears on the formulation of policy. It is the purpose of the series to make the findings of this research available to those who are responsible for raising a new generation and for shaping policy in its behalf. We hope that these books will provide rich and useful information for parents, educators, child-care professionals, students of developmental psychology, and all others concerned with the challenge of human growth.

Jerome Bruner
New York University
Michael Cole
University of California, San Diego
SERIES EDITORS

The Developing Child Series

Early Literacy

Joan Brooks McLane
Gillian Dowley McNamee

Harvard University Press
Cambridge, Massachusetts
London, England   1990

This book is printed on acid-free paper, and its binding materials have
been chosen for strength and durability.

Library of Congress Cataloging-in-Publication Data

McLane, Joan Brooks.
    Early literacy / Joan Brooks McLane, Gillian Dowley McNamee.
        p.   cm.—(The developing child)
    Includes bibliographical references.
    ISBN 0-674-22164-8(alk. paper).—ISBN 0-674-22165-6 (pbk. : alk. paper)
    1. Children—Language. 2. Language acquisition. 3. Language arts
(Preschool) 4. Literacy. 5. Education, Preschool—Parent participation.
I. McNamee, Gillian Dowley, 1951–   . II. Title. III. Series.
LB1139.L3M3348   1990
372.6—dc20   89-27082
                                                                  CIP

Acknowledgments

This book includes many voices, and our debts are numerous. The greatest is to Robert Gundlach, who has served as consultant and colleague for much of our work, and who has contributed a great deal to our understanding of early literacy, particularly early writing development. Many of his ideas are reflected in this book. Indeed, much of our work grew out of our attempt to answer questions he posed several years ago after we read Glenda Bissex's *Gnys at Wrk*, an extended case study of one child's learning to write and read that begins when Paul Bissex is 5 years old and starting to invent his own spellings. How, Bob Gundlach asked, does a 5-year-old get to the point of being able to construct more or less interpretable written messages, and why, considering the complexity and difficulty of the enterprise, would a young child want to do this? What motivates young children to experiment with writing and reading well before school, and what kind of supports do children find for their early efforts to use and make sense of written language? How do writing and reading come to have a significant place in young children's lives?

To help in answering these questions, a number of parents, teachers, and program administrators allowed us to observe and work with them and their children. Several parents contributed detailed and thoughtful written observations of their children's writing and reading activities, and shared their insights about this process with us. Many of these parents and children appear in the book, (usually with their names changed). We are especially grateful to Caroline Bell, Nancy Lany, Carl and Jane Smith, Arphalia Todd, and Jean Ward.

People at three Hull House Association sites in Chicago—Clarence Darrow Community Center, Uptown Family Care, and Uptown Head Start—have worked in close partnership with us over the past six years. Their concern for their children, their children's education, and how to ensure the best for them, inspired us to pass on to them and to others what we have learned about where literacy begins and how it can develop in the early years of children's lives. We have great respect and gratitude for the efforts of the staff and parents in these community centers, and we thank them for their openness and willingness to work with us.

Several colleagues read and commented on parts of the manuscript at various stages, and we are grateful for their comments, criticisms, and insights: Terry and Lynn Chadsey, Deirdre Graziano, Bonnie Litowitz, Vivian Paley, Frances M. Stott, Kiki Wilson, the editors of the Developing Child Series, Jerome Bruner and Michael Cole, and our editors at Harvard University Press, Angela von der Lippe and Camille Smith. The faculty and staff at Erikson Institute gave us intellectual support, encouragement, and invaluable technical assistance in preparing the manuscript.

A number of foundations have supported various phases of our work with teachers and parents, including the Borg Warner Foundation, Chicago Tribune Charities, the Field Foundation of Illinois, the Field Corporation Fund, the Foundation for Children With Learning Disabilities, the Lloyd Fry Foundation, General Service Foundation, Irving B. Harris, the Kellogg Foundation, Northern Trust Company, the Anne S. Richardson Fund, the Spencer Foundation, and the Woods Charitable Fund. We are grateful for their recognition of the importance of understanding the beginnings of literacy and their interest in what might be done to help give children a strong start in becoming literate.

Finally, our husbands, Jock and Michael, encouraged us throughout the writing of this, our first book, which is dedicated to them.

Contents

Photo Credits

The
Developing
Child

Early Literacy

1 / What Is Literacy?

When he was 4 years old, Joshua made up a writing game by inventing a variation on a familiar family routine. In the basic format, Joshua's mother would challenge him to do something before she counted to a certain number: "Get into the bathtub before I count to four"; "Pick up the toys before I get to ten." One day while he was getting dressed Joshua told his mother: "See if you can write 'pencil' before I put my shirt on." He looked around the room to find words for her to write, trying to find long ones for the more complicated articles of clothing—"bear" was for his socks, "Christmas tree" for his sweatshirt.

Later that day Joshua reversed the roles when he wanted his father to come downstairs: "See if you can get downstairs before I write 'to,' " he called, and then dashed into his room. A minute later he came out, having written OT (on the same piece of paper his mother had used earlier). Joshua was delighted: "I did it! See the letters? I wrote it myself!" His mother commented that his "triumph here was divided between winning the race and writing the letters."

Joshua's game makes it clear that he is very interested in writing. He does not yet know how to write, but he pretends to know. Playing with writing is one way he learns about written language and how it can be used. The kinds of make-believe writing and reading children bring into their play can tell us a great deal about how and when literacy begins.

There are many disputes and unresolved questions about how literacy develops. Indeed, literacy itself is not easy to define. One definition is knowing the letters of the alphabet and how to use them to read and write. But, as Frederick Erickson has noted, "to be *lettered* means more than this."[1] The "more than this" is not easy to pin down, but it involves attitudes, assumptions, and expectations about writing and reading, and about the place and value of these activities in one's life. Literacy is a complex and multifaceted phenomenon.

Central to many recent discussions of literacy is the notion that writing and reading are ways of making, interpreting, and communicating meaning. Reading is defined as the ability to "take meaning from print,"[2] and writing as the ability to use print to communicate with others. According to these definitions, reading and writing are more than simply decoding and encoding print: they are ways of constructing and conveying meaning with written language.

Recent research also suggests that literacy is not a monolithic, all-or-nothing affair. In modern westernized societies such as our own, it may not be realistic to describe people as "literate" or "illiterate," partly because very few people are completely "nonliterate."[3] That is, most adults, even those whose writing and reading skills are minimal, recognize some forms of print and know something about how print is used. In contemporary societies, print seems to be everywhere—on newspapers, magazines, books, food, and household products, in advertisements, on street signs and billboards, and on TV. Clearly, not all people read and write with equal ease and fluency or use writing and reading in the same ways or for the same purposes. In the long run, it may be useful to think of "multiple literacies."[4] The notion of multiple literacies recognizes that there are many ways of being—and of becoming—literate, and that how literacy develops and how it is used depend on the particular social and cultural setting. Literacy is a social and cultural achievement, as well as a cognitive one.

When adults write and read, they do so for specific reasons and purposes. In examining the ways in which literacy functions in people's everyday lives, we begin to uncover their reasons for writing and reading, and their motivations for learning to do so in the first place. Learning to read and write is a difficult and lengthy undertaking, and children and adults often work hard at mastering it. Their reasons for doing so are tied to their uses for writing and reading, and to the meaning of these activities in their everyday lives.

In our view, literacy is both an individual intellectual achievement and a form of cultural knowledge that enables people to participate in a range of groups and activities that in some way involve writing and reading. It is closely tied to specific relationships and specific social and cultural contexts and activities.

To understand the development of literacy, we must study the environments in which young children develop, and the ways in which these settings provide opportunities for children to become involved with books, paper, and writing tools. The environment includes not only physical surroundings but also human relationships, which determine when, how often, and in what situations children are introduced to the tools, materials, uses, and meanings of literacy. In some cultures, literacy development is closely tied to schooling, but for many children in modern westernized societies, literacy begins long before formal education, in the home and in other community settings such as preschools, daycare centers, and churches.

EARLY LITERACY

This is not a book about how to teach very young children to read and write. Rather, it is about the beginnings of literacy and the processes by which young children become literate. One of our major goals is to demonstrate that the development of literacy consists of more than learning skills such as handwriting, decoding, and spelling. Rather, literacy development consists of mastering a complex set of attitudes, expectations, feelings, behaviors, and skills related to written language. This collection of attitudes and skills constitutes what has been called "emergent literacy."[5] There is a growing body of evidence that early—or emergent—literacy often begins well before children go to school and before they master the technical skills involved in writing and reading. We will review some of this evidence in an effort to identify what happens in the early years of children's lives that can help them build a foundation for mature literacy.

For many children, the beginnings of literacy appear in activities such as pretend play, drawing, conversations about storybook plots and characters, and conversations about the words on street signs or the labels of favorite foods. Such activities make it clear that children are actively trying to use—and to understand and make sense of—reading and writing long before they can actually read and write. As they experiment with written language, often in playful ways, children begin to learn what writing and reading are, and what they can do with them. At the same time, they acquire a broad range of knowledge, attitudes, and skills related to writing and reading.

Writing and reading are intimately related, and clearly depend on one another: "The efforts of a writer are always partially governed by the anticipated needs and desires of the reader, and of course a reader's efforts are always partially directed by the purposes and interests of the writer . . . To succeed in one role requires some understanding of the other."[6] But writing and reading are not simply two sides of the same coin; in many ways, they are quite distinct pursuits.

Early writing activities tend to be more visible than early reading activities because they involve making something—usually marks on paper. As young children scribble and draw, they often begin to experiment with making wavy lines and letterlike shapes. They frequently mix writing and drawing, creating what Robert Gundlach has termed a "mixed medium" that combines graphic forms, letters, and words. In these early experiments, children begin to realize that writing can be useful in their social relationships: they can use writing to make requests, to define and label their world, to express feelings of friendship and anger, to get attention, and so forth. When children play with the activity of writing, with the role of writer, and with the materials used to create written texts, they begin to learn how to form letters and write words, often inventing their own spellings in the process, and how to construct literary forms such as notes, letters, stories, and poems.

Reading involves a less visible, more internal mental process, but young children engage in a range of activities that indicate that they are trying to understand and participate in reading. They act out the role of reader, they include books and pretend reading in their dramatic play, and they include plots and characters from storybooks in their fantasy and pretend play. In enacting the role of reader, many children learn to give precise, accurate "readings" of their favorite storybooks long before they can decode print. As children's awareness of print develops, they begin to recognize—and to read—letters and familiar words that they encounter in books and on cereal boxes, stop signs, buses, and countless other places in their environment.

Possibly the most important reading activity for young children is being read to. A considerable body of research has confirmed the link between being read to and later learning to read successfully in school. As children are read to, they acquire an enormous amount of information about reading and the world of books. They learn what books are, what you do with them, and how you talk about them. They learn that written words can create imaginary worlds beyond the immediate here-and-now. They learn that written language has its own rhythms and conventions. They learn about specific features of written language: for example, that the black marks on the page are letters and words, and that print goes from left to right and from top to bottom on the page. And they come to expect that books will be interesting, challenging, exciting, and comforting.

WHEN DOES LITERACY BEGIN?

If literacy is a cultural, social, and cognitive achievement, when does its development begin? For some children, learning to write and to read appears to happen spontaneously and "naturally," and sometimes well before formal schooling. Some children begin to read simple picture books and to write words such as their own names, names of family members, and names of their favorite toys or places, and some even compose sentences, stories, and poems during the preschool years. At first glance it might appear that these achievements are similar to other kinds of maturational or biological development—they seem to occur without any special intervention from the environment. However, early literacy development does not just happen. Close observation of children's early literacy activities suggests that children are likely to become interested in writing and reading when they observe and participate in these activities with more competent writers and readers—especially with parents and older brothers and sisters.

The development of literacy, then, is a profoundly social process, embedded in social relationships, particularly in children's relationships with parents, siblings, grandparents, friends, caretakers, and teachers. These people serve as models, provide materials, establish expectations, and offer help, instruction, and encouragement. Literacy development begins in children's relationships with their immediate caretakers, and is expressed and elaborated in increasingly wider communities—at home, in the neighborhood, and in preschool, daycare, and kindergarten settings.

There is considerable variation in patterns of early

literacy development because there are differences in the ways writing and reading are organized in different communities, and because writing and reading serve different functions in people's day to day lives. Writing and reading are a central part of some people's professional lives, while for others, writing and reading may be used primarily for practical purposes such as remembering what to buy at the grocery store. This means that children encounter differing resources, and differing kinds and degrees of support for early literacy development. For example, some children may have ready access to a range of writing and reading materials, while others do not; some children observe their parents writing and reading frequently, others only occasionally; some children receive direct, didactic instruction in writing and reading from their parents, while other children receive much more casual, informal assistance, sometimes in the context of playful interactions centered around writing and reading.

Activities such as pretend play, drawing, and being read to can nurture and influence children's understanding of what the system of written language is all about. Children can use these experiences to make connections and build "bridges" to the activities of writing and reading. Joshua's "writing game" reflects many of these themes. This game was invented in the context of Joshua's relationship with his parents, in response to a family routine. Writing and reading are an integral part of Joshua's parents' personal and professional lives, and these activities enter into their relationship with their son in many ways. In the context of this relationship, and as part of his daily routines, Joshua frequently experiments with writing and reading, using them for a variety of playful and communicative purposes. For Joshua, this writing game represents one of many opportunities to try out and practice what *he* thinks it means to write and read, and to experience the confidence, joy, and power associated with mastering these complex and important activities.

2 / Bridges to Literacy

A child's first steps toward literacy may not look much like adult activities such as reading a book or writing a letter, but rather may consist of talking, drawing, or playing. Many years ago the Soviet psychologist Lev Vygotsky noted that "make-believe play, drawing, and writing can be viewed as different moments in an essentially unified process of development of written language." More recently, Anne Dyson pointed out that researchers should look for the beginnings of literacy in "all kinds of making that children do." Drawing, playing, and talking are all symbolic activities, and it is in these activities that the beginnings of writing and reading can be found. Children can use these early symbolic activities to build "bridges" to literacy.[1]

Between the ages of 1 and 5, children learn to use symbols to create and communicate meaning—both symbols they invent for themselves and those "donated by the culture."[2] The use of symbols—which may include words, gestures, marks on paper, objects modeled in clay, and so forth—makes it possible to represent experiences, feelings, and ideas. Symbols also allow children to go beyond the immediate here and now and to create imaginary worlds. This is what they do when

11

they make up stories, engage in pretend play, or draw images on paper—and, later, when they read books and write stories.

As children begin to experiment with writing and reading, they may find them useful in some of the same ways as their other symbolic activities. It is in this way that their earlier forms of communication such as play, talk, and drawing can serve as bridges to literacy, as children discover that writing and reading offer them new and interesting resources for communicating meaning.

A MIXED MEDIUM

To most adults, talk, play, and drawing appear to be quite different kinds of symbolic media, with different forms and different functions. But children do not necessarily make the same distinctions that adults do, and many preschool children find a variety of ways to combine drawing, talking, and pretend play into one coherent "mixed medium," which they use to create and express meaning.[3]

For example, 3½-year-old Molly made a drawing and then used it as part of a dramatic pretend play production. She drew an M shape, which she then turned into a rabbit's face (see Figures 1 and 2). Using different voices, facial expressions, and gestures, she then transformed this simple drawing into the central character in a pretend play narrative about "Flopsy, the talking rabbit."[4]

In using the first letter of her own name as the basis for her drawing-story-drama about one of the characters from *Peter Rabbit*, Molly was using a culturally agreed upon symbol in a personally meaningful way. Her dra-

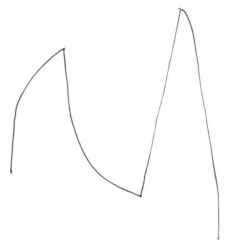

Figure 1. "An M . . . What does that spell? It spells M for Molly."

Figure 2. "And it could be a rabbit. See, it's got big ears. One, two. It's Flopsy, the talking rabbit. Flopsy, Mopsy, and Cottontail. . . . [holding up the paper, speaking in a tiny voice] Hello, I'm Flopsy, the talking rabbit, and I live with my brothers in a tiny house in the forest."

matic production illustrates the richness and variety with which some young children combine drawing, writing, talking, and pretend play to create imaginary worlds and to express personal meaning through the symbols the culture makes available to them.

Many children conduct similar playful explorations throughout the preschool and early elementary years, creating a mixed medium in which bits of writing are surrounded and supported by talk, gestures, or drawing. As they experiment with various ways of using symbols, children gradually learn to differentiate symbolic media as they learn what is unique about the forms and functions of talk, gestures, lines on paper.

PLAY

Play consumes much of young children's time and energy, and for many children, play is where writing and reading begin. Play is the arena in which young children make connections between their immediate personal world and activities that are important in the larger social world of family and community, and play is the context in which many children find ways to make culturally valued activities part of their own personal experience.

Probably the most useful way to think about play is as an attitude toward or approach to experience, and as a way of doing things, rather than as any particular set of behaviors. According to Jerome Bruner, "Play is an approach to action, not a form of activity." This approach involves some understanding that the action is nonliteral or "not for real," an understanding that can be seen most clearly in pretend or make-believe play, but that permeates all forms of play.[5] In the safety of pretend play, children can learn about the tools, materials, activities, and roles of their culture, and can do so on their own terms.

Play appears to have at least two potential links to the development of literacy: (1) As a symbolic activity, pretend play allows children to develop and refine their capacities to use symbols, to represent experience, and to construct imaginary worlds, capacities they will draw on when they begin to write and read. (2) As an orientation or approach to experience, play can make the various roles and activities of people who read and write more meaningful and hence more accessible to young children.

PRETEND PLAY AND IMAGINARY WORLDS

Pretend play—or make-believe or dramatic or symbolic play—involves the use of symbols to create an imaginary situation. Pretend play allows children a wide choice of symbolic vehicles, including sounds, gestures, and speech as well as objects and persons (both self and others), which can be imaginatively transformed to represent meanings. Imaginary situations are created by giving things, places, and people temporary identities, pretending they are something other than what they really are. In pretend play children can impose their own ideas and meanings on objects and use them as they please. Thus, a wooden building block can become a doll's bed, a witch's broom, a police car, or a wild animal, and a bedroom can become a house, a witch's hideaway, a police station, or a jungle—whatever the child wants them to be. And children can also become whatever they want to be, taking on the roles of mother, father, witch, lion, monster, hero. Howard Gardner has noted that in early pretend play the "achievement of symbolic activity is enormous—in a sense, the greatest leap of all. Upon it will be constructed all subsequent forms of play, including the play of literary imagination."[6]

When children create imaginary situations in pretend play, they invent and inhabit "alternative" or "possible" worlds. This is similar to what they do when they listen to storybooks, and to what they do when they read or write stories themselves. Indeed, there are similarities between pretend play and storytelling, and in the kinds of competence the two require.[7] Many children make up their first stories in the context of pretend play, creating and enacting their own dramatic narratives (and reenacting favorite stories they have heard being read aloud). Indeed, one of the things that attracts young children to pretend play is the chance to tell stories. Later, many children are attracted to writing and reading for the same reasons: they find they can use writing to tell stories, and that by reading they can participate in stories told by others.

As children mature, their pretend play and the symbolic transformations they use to create and sustain it become increasingly elaborate, complex, and abstract. With development, pretend play becomes less dependent on physical props, gestures, and actions, and relies increasingly on ideas, imagination, and language. Children often employ abundant, rich language in pretend play. An increasing proportion of the time devoted to pretend play is spent in talk, as children discuss the setting, the characters or roles, and the plots they will enact in their play. Indeed, at times it seems as though "the saying is the playing."[8] As pretend play becomes increasingly dependent on language to create possible worlds and to express and communicate meanings, it comes closer to the experiences of storytelling, writing, and reading.

PLAYING WITH WRITING AND READING

Children seem to be able to play with almost anything: objects, movements, behaviors, roles, rules, and language. Many play with the implements and materials of written language: with paper, pencils, markers, crayons, and books, with the activities of writing and reading, and with the roles of writer and reader. Children incorporate both real and pretend writing and reading into their dramatic play, using them to enhance the drama and realism of the pretend situation. They may use characters and plots from their favorite storybooks. Some preschool children explore the tools and activities of literacy in playful ways, using pretend writing to create "stories," "poems," or "news bulletins"—as 4½-year-old Joshua did one Sunday afternoon: After dressing up in various costumes and pretending he was "a baby learning to fly," Joshua wrote some letters and letterlike figures on a piece of paper. He showed this to his mother and said "Now wait for the surprise." Then he held the paper in front of his face while he shouted: "Good evening ladies and gentlemen! This is the ABC News! Now we have lots of weather!"

Joshua's written news report and his reading of it contain elements of real literacy—letterlike shapes, and the understanding that these carry a message. In this sort of play children practice and integrate what they know or what they surmise about a range of activities and roles outside their immediate experience and understanding. As Greta Fein observed, "pretense [may] provide special opportunities for the partially under-stood and the dimly grasped to become more firmly mastered."[9] By playing with writing and reading, chil-dren become familiar with the tools of literacy and begin to learn how to use and control them. Such play also allows children to acquire some global notions of what writing and reading consist of and what they can do with them.

In play the focus is on exploring rather than on ac-complishing predetermined ends or goals, so there are few pressures to produce correct answers or final prod-ucts. Play's nonliteral, not-for-real, "not-for-profit" ori-entation allows players the freedom to manipulate materials, experiences, roles, and ideas in new, creative, experimental, "as if" ways. Play thus creates a risk-free context in which children do not have to worry about "getting it right" or about "messing up." This free-dom may lead children to discover or invent new possibilities—new ways of doing things and new ways of thinking about ideas—which may, in turn, lead them to new questions, problems, and solutions. Approach-ing writing and reading with such an experimental, "as if" attitude may help children realize that written lan-guage is something they can manipulate in a variety of ways and for a variety of purposes. Playing at writing and reading—by scribbling, drawing, pretending to write, or pretending to read—may serve to open up the activities of writing and reading for children's consider-ation and exploration.[10]

Pretend play often involves reversals of everyday, real-life roles and power relationships. When they pre-tend, children can enact powerful roles such as mother, father, doctor, fireman, witch, monster, writer, and reader and take on the competencies that come with these roles, as Joshua did when he "wrote" and "read" the "ABC News." In doing this, Joshua assumed the confidence and power of someone who can write and read, and engaged in writing and reading on his own terms, defining them as he was able to carry them out at the moment.

Play thus encourages children to act *as if* they are already competent in and able to control the activity under consideration: they can act as if they know how to cook, put out fires, kill monsters, read books, or write stories. Playing with the roles of writer and reader can give children a sense of ownership of these roles. Through play, children may come to feel that they are writers and readers long before they actually have the necessary skills and knowledge to write and read. The sense of accomplishment such play can give shows in Joshua's playful assertion (quoted in Chapter 1): "I did it! See the letters! I wrote it myself!" Such feelings of competence and control are likely to nourish assumptions and expectations about becoming literate, and to give children the motivation to work at learning to write and read.

While activities like talking, playing, and drawing are closely linked to writing and reading, and while their uses often intertwine and overlap, there are not direct or inevitable transitions between earlier- and later-developed symbol systems. Whether and how children make connections between talking, playing, drawing, and writing and reading depends on the children's interests and personalities, on what is available and valued in their particular culture, *and* on how the adults around them treat writing and reading. Children's capacity to use symbols is engaged by people who model and demonstrate their use, who involve children in symbol-using activities, who encourage children to use symbols in a variety of ways, and who give children materials with which to explore, experiment, and play.

3 / Writing

In many ways, writing is the neglected half of literacy. It has received far less attention from researchers than reading, and we know less about the relationship between early experience and later success in school for writing than we do for reading. Most primary-grade teachers give more time and attention to teaching reading than to teaching writing, and writing instruction is often limited to worksheet exercises in handwriting and spelling. During the last several years, however, there has been increasing interest in the early development of writing, both in and out of school, and in new approaches to the teaching of writing in the primary grades. Both of these areas of inquiry stress the importance of looking at what children *do* with writing, and of considering writing as a process rather than as a collection of skills such as handwriting and spelling.

When children learn to write, what are they learning to do? Robert Gundlach has argued that beginning writers are learning to master (1) the functions, uses, and purposes of writing, (2) the forms and features of written language, and (3) the processes of writing.[1] Children must learn what writing can do, and, in particular, what they can do with writing. They must learn what writing looks like—its distinctive orthographic features and the various forms of written products, such as lists, stories, and poems. And they must learn how writing is produced. If their environments encourage them to experiment with writing materials, children begin to master each of these dimensions of writing long before they are able to produce messages that are generally readable or interpretable by others.

The *function* of writing is perhaps the least studied, least understood, and most interesting of the three dimensions. When young children write before school and outside of school, what is their writing *for?* What are their reasons for writing? Writing is not easy for a beginner; given the difficulties, why do young children choose to write? The writing activities that children engage in before school and outside of school often function as part of other activities in their lives, such as speaking, drawing, and playing.

The *forms* and *features* of written language—what one sees on the page—are a more familiar dimension. Mastering the formal aspects of writing involves learning at many levels: learning how to form letters and spell words, learning when to capitalize and how to punctuate, learning the conventions of grammar, and learning about different literary genres such as stories, poems, and essays.

The *process* of writing is complex. As experienced writers know, a great deal of organization and management goes into getting ideas onto paper. When young children begin to write, adults (and sometimes older siblings and friends) are often involved in the process. They can serve as models, scribes, and friendly editors, as well as responsive listeners and readers, so that beginning writers do not have to understand or manage all the complexities of writing on their own.

Much of children's early writing does not look like

"real" writing. This is particularly true of the pretend writing produced by many children between the ages of 2 and 5, which often consists of a mixture of scribbles, letterlike shapes, and random arrangements of recognizable letters. Writing in which children employ "invented spelling" may be easier than pretend writing for other people to interpret, but it often requires some oral explication by the writer. Because of this, much early writing is closely tied to the contexts in which it is produced, and can only be read and understood in these contexts. For example, much of the writing produced by preschool children is interpretable only when it is surrounded and supported by speech—when the authors are there in person to explain their writing to their audience. Such early writing does not serve as a substitute for speech; rather, it serves as an accompaniment to speech, an extension and elaboration of speech. Only gradually do young children produce writing that is able to stand on its own and communicate at a distance, over time and space.

LEARNING USES FOR WRITING

As children find uses for writing, they become attached to what they can do with it, and thus they are likely to be motivated to learn about its forms and processes in order to use it more effectively. In other words, learning uses for writing can be particularly important in motivating children's writing development. A sample of writing activities engaged in before school and outside of school suggests that in supportive environments young children do find ways of using writing to pursue their own interests and purposes. These interests are often related to play, fantasy, or pretending; to drawing; or to making contact with other people—

parents, siblings, friends—who are important to the young writers.

PLAYING WITH WRITING

Children as young as 2 and 3 include writing and reading—what they identify as writing and reading—in their pretend play, using these activities to embellish the dramatic action or to give the roles they are acting out greater credibility and power. Thus we see young policemen, train conductors, waitresses, hairdressers, mothers, TV announcers, circus impresarios, librarians, bookstore managers—writing traffic tickets, train tickets, grocery lists, telephone messages, menus, programs, bills, receipts, library cards. Children have been observed making "sleeping charts" (to determine when it was the turn of a particular doll or stuffed animal to sleep in the child's bed) and writing adoption papers for a doll. Children also use written signs and labels to enhance their fantasy play, as 5-year-old Paul Bissex did when he put the following sign on the door of a cabinet in his room:

PAULZ RABR SAF RABRZ KANT GT EN
(Paul's robber safe. Robbers can't get in.)

When children bring writing into their play in these ways, it indicates that they recognize writing as an activity worth imitating and experimenting with, and that they are seeking ways to make this activity serve their own purposes.[2]

On other occasions, children engage in writing that is playful in spirit—playful in the sense that it is freely chosen by the child and under the child's control, and playful because it is carried out in a nonliteral, experimental manner. It seems likely that Jerome Bruner's notion that young children's use of language (while they

are acquiring it) "is most daring and most advanced
when it is used in a playful setting" applies not only to
spoken language but to written language acquisition as
well.[3]

Young writers experiment with the visual features,
formats, and conventions of written language, exploring the way language looks on the page, sometimes
using different colors, different kinds of handwriting,
and different spatial arrangements for letters and words.
For example, at age 4½ Joshua used his typewriter to
compose the following poem on three small pieces of
paper:

U U U U P
JJ 1 '''
J J J J J J. . . . . .

When he read the poem to his mother he explained that
the marks on the second page were "bullets making gun
noises." Karla, age 6, wrote her own variation on an old
favorite, using an appropriately colored marker for each
line:

Roses are red
Violets are blue
Flowers are purple
Pumpkins are orange
The skys are blue
Grass is green
Shoes are black.

Both Joshua and Karla were playfully experimenting
with literary forms already available to them: Joshua's
parents had read poetry to him, and Karla had heard
her school friends recite the rhyme beginning "Roses
are red, violets are blue" (which has been given many
different endings over the years). Such playful explora-

tion is one way children can learn about literary forms as they discover what can be done with them.

Children also play with other conventional forms of writing, such as signs and lists. For example, Bissex observed that Paul, at age 5, wrote a number of "pseudo shopping lists" such as this one:

> SHAP.ING.LETS. (shopping list)
> 5000 BATLZ.AV.WESKY. (bottles of whiskey)
> AND 100 BATLZ.AV.BER. (bottles of beer)
> AND. 5000 BAGZ.AV.DOG FOD (bags of dog
> food). (p. 25)

These uses of written language are similar to children's play with spoken language. When children play with oral language, they treat words, sounds, and meanings as objects to be experimented with. Courtney Cazden has argued that play with spoken language helps children develop "metalinguistic awareness"—the understanding that language is a system of sounds and meanings that can be manipulated and used in a variety of ways.[4] It seems likely that play with writing helps children develop an understanding that written language, too, can be manipulated—an awareness of what can be done with it, and in particular of what *they* can do with it.

DRAWING AND WRITING

For many young children, drawing and writing are closely linked, serving as equivalent and complementary means of self-expression. Many preschool and kindergarten children make graphic products that combine letters or letterlike shapes and words with representational and nonrepresentational drawing and painting. This "mixed medium" is often informed by a spirit of playful manipulation and experimentation.[5] For example, when Joshua was about 4½ he made a number of what he called "pictures with letters"—large pieces of paper covered with letters of different colors arranged in rows or patterns. Once he made what he called a "drawing with rhymes": on a large piece of paper he drew scribbles, a strange shape, the letters O A O A A J and bp, and a picture of a stick figure holding something. He explained that this drawing included the following rhymes:

J and A
A O and A O (read from right to left)
O and toe (the strange shape was a toe with a jagged toenail)
b and p
Raggedy Andy holding candy (the stick figure).

Joshua had combined drawing and writing by rhyming letters with each other, letters with pictures of objects, and pictures with other pictures. Here, drawing and writing are intricately—and playfully—mixed together.

Young children combine drawing and writing in many different ways, and sometimes use the two interchangeably to convey meaning. Often children who are beginning to use conventional writing will use writing to label, identify, and explain their drawings, and use drawing to explain or elaborate on their writing. Some children's earliest written stories are mostly drawing, probably because drawing is more familiar and easier to control than writing. For example, when 6-year-old Jose, a child in an after-school daycare program, composed his first story, it consisted of brightly colored drawings of four figures, each with a caption over its head bearing the name of one of the four adults involved in the program: Ana, Deborah, Joan, and Deirdre. Underneath this drawing, Jose wrote, "They were walking down the road." The picture was as important as the printed words in conveying the author's meaning.

WRITING AND SOCIAL RELATIONSHIPS

Glenda Bissex, who conducted an extended case study of her son's writing development between the ages of 5 and 10, began her account with an anecdote: At age 5, Paul was trying to engage her in conversation while she was reading a book. When he was unsuccessful, he took rubber letter stamps and "printed and delivered this message: RUDF (Are you deaf?!)." Bissex noted, "Of course, I put down my book." Paul had found an effective way to get his mother's attention: he had managed "to break through print with print" (p. 3).

Like Paul, many young children learn that they can do things with writing that they could not do with speaking alone. Many children begin to use bits and pieces of writing—what they define as writing—to communicate with family members and friends: to mark holidays and special occasions, to make requests, to set limits, to express affection or anger, to amuse or provoke, to get attention. When children do this, and discover that it works, they begin to realize that writing offers them a potent way to communicate with other people. This realization, in turn, fuels their interest in learning more about written language.

Making requests. Children find they can use writing to request favors and privileges from parents and siblings, as well as from magical figures such as the Tooth Fairy and Santa Claus. For example, when she was 3½, Rachel typed a random string of letters that she said was a note to her father. She read it as: "Dear Daddy, Happy birthday. I love you. I want to play with that computer. I will send you a present." A promise to send a present is appropriate in a birthday message, but a request is not. Rachel may have felt that inserting her request to use the computer in a birthday letter would make it more acceptable than presenting it in isolation. She also may have felt that putting it in writing would give it more status and authority, increasing the likelihood of a favorable response. When a 6-year-old girl wanted to stay up past her bedtime to see the end of a television special, she wrote a note to her mother:

To Mom
Please let me
stay up because
if i don't see the
program now, I will
never get the
chance to see it.
it's now or *never*
yes no
circle
yes.

This young writer managed to use writing to present a reasoned and persuasive argument; moreover, the fact that she put her request in writing probably made it more compelling to her mother, who appreciated her daughter's writing efforts—and granted her request.[6]

A 7-year-old boy wrote the following note on an envelope and put it under his pillow:

Don't take my
touth I'v had
it since
I was ten days old.

In this case, writing may have seemed the best—if not the only—way to communicate with an elusive character like the Tooth Fairy, who is not available for face-to-face encounters. This child took advantage of the permanence of written language, which makes it possible to communicate at a distance.[7]

Makings signs and labels. Many young children use writing to label and define their world, making signs and captions to put on their possessions and on the walls and doors of their bedrooms. In part, as Bissex observed of her son, such writing may serve the child's interest "in knowing his world by naming its parts" (p. 101). Signs and labels can also serve to announce and assert ownership, to define spheres of influence and set territorial limits—particularly on the encroachments of siblings. Many children put signs on their bedroom doors, such as 5½-year-old Joshua's DO NOT ENTER and 6-year-old Paul's series of signs:

GO AWAY
LEVE ME ALON
GET LOST
DON'T BOTER ME
NEVER MIND
GET OUT
BUG OFF.   (p. 53)

Five-year-old Stephen was bothered by frequent interruptions from his older brother and sister while his mother read him his nightly bedtime story. One night, with some exasperation, he said to his mother, "I really want a sign on my door." The next day she helped him make a round target-like sign with a movable arrow in the center. The sign was divided into eight pie-shaped segments, four of them filled in with the following messages:

STAY OUT
COME IN
ASK ME IF YOU HEAR ME PLAYING WHETHER I

WANT YOU TO COME IN OR STAY OUT
YOU CAN COME IN IF MOM IS READING BUT ONLY
ASK ONE QUESTION.

Stephen hung the sign on his bedroom door. His mother commented that although Stephen didn't use the sign much, he was very satisfied with it and kept it on his door for months.

Joshua, Paul, and Stephen are learning that they can use writing to assert their rights and to set limits on others—they are learning that "putting it in writing" makes the message more effective and powerful than simply saying it; not only does writing make the message permanent, it also conveys the message with the authority and prestige of an important adult means of communication. Moreover, children may find that when they write they are allowed to use more forceful language than when they speak—utterances that would be considered rude if spoken are sometimes acceptable in print.

Expressing anger. Some children discover they can use writing to communicate strong feelings that might be difficult—or dangerous—to express in face-to-face encounters. Frances Stott reported on such an incident: One evening 5-year-old Jill's older sister, Nina, went to spend the night at a friend's house. Jill, feeling left out, was irritable all evening. When her mother told her it was time for her to go to bed, she objected, arguing that Nina was probably staying up late. But her mother insisted that she go to bed and sent Jill upstairs to her room. Some time later, thirteen small pieces of paper came fluttering down the stairs, each bearing the same message: I HAT YOU. This "rain of hate" offers a vivid example of the powerful feelings that can be put into written words, as well as the distance and safety that writing can provide. Jill had discovered that a writer can compose a message and deliver it in a way that avoids the risk of face-to-face confrontation.[8]

Writing among friends. Between the ages of 5 and 7, children become increasingly interested in relationships with their peers, and for some, writing can be useful in conducting these relationships. Joan McLane and Deirdre Graziano initiated informal writing activities in an after-school daycare program for inner-city 6-, 7-, and 8-year-olds.[9] These children had had little experience with writing other than copying words and sentences from the blackboard and filling in workbooks at school. Once they realized that they were expected to write—and that they were free to write whatever they wanted—they began experimenting with writing as a means of offering friendship, cementing alliances, and declaring hostility. They wrote to and about each other, to the researchers, and to the group workers in charge of the program. They wrote notes of friendship, lists of friends, and stories about each other and the adults involved in the program.

As the children grew more comfortable with writing, they began using it in increasingly provocative ways, writing playful tests and challenges to the adults and jokes and insults to each other. For example, 7-year-old Maria (who speaks Spanish at home) wrote a "test" for one of the researchers (the test was to guess a particular number):

DEIRDARE IS NOT GOIG TO GESS IT _____ .

Maria challenged the other researcher as follows:

I Love all the
Techers epset Joan
Ha Ha Ha for you I am
jest kidteing Joan
So you Better Not

feal good if you
Do you are going
to get it OK"
HA" HA" HA"
lets see if you know
thes numbers uno dos
trees cuatro if you do
NOT know it you ar Not
The Techer.

Maria appeared to take great pleasure in playfully reversing roles with the adults in the program (all of whom were categorized by the children as "teachers").

Eight-year-old Rosa initiated an interchange of insulting stories between the girls and the boys with THREE LITTLE SCARY CATS. The protagonists in her story were three boys in the group, whom she portrayed as "little scary cats" who were "scared of the dark, a cat, a dog, a little bird, and a little baby." The three boys were, of course, outraged when Rosa's story was read aloud. One of them, 7-year-old Kevin, responded by putting Rosa and two other girls into a story in which they became THE LIVIG DEAD, all of whom were eaten. He later wrote about them again as THE PIGS THAT LIKED MUD. Gradually, the insults grew more direct; for example, Maria wrote:

KARLA IS DUM . . . SHE DOES NOT KNOW HER
TAIM TABLES.

These children had discovered that writing allowed them a certain distance and safety to express ideas and feelings that might be embarrassing or risky to say. This point was illustrated most vividly when one child flung an insult she had written at the feet of the intended recipient and hastily retreated to another part of the room.

However, when the insults went too far for some of the adults, the children learned that putting ideas in writing may also entail some risk. This was illustrated when Oscar, a 6-year-old with poor writing skills but with great interest in writing, wrote a note to Ana, the group worker he was most attached to. He asked a researcher how to spell "nosey" and then wrote NOSEY ANA on a scrap of paper and handed it to Ana. (When asked why Ana was "nosey," he said "because she looks too much.") Ana was offended by the note and told Oscar to write her an apology. He then wrote a note saying SORRY ANA, and gave it to Ana, who said "Thank you, Oscar." In this case, the adult was also using writing to manage social relationships in the group.

Within the small community of the after-school program, the children were discovering uses for writing that *they* found interesting. In the process, they were learning that writing could be an effective and powerful means of expressing and asserting themselves, of pleasing, amusing, provoking, offending, and apologizing. This may be particularly important for children who have few opportunities either at home or at school to discover their own uses for writing. When children's experience with writing is restricted to classroom exercises in handwriting and spelling, it is much harder for them to understand the potential power of writing in their own lives, and much harder for them to develop a sense of potential control and authorship.

When children come to value what they can do with writing, they are likely to want to learn more about it, and to want to develop their competence as writers. This is worth emphasizing because it is not immediately obvious why young children might want to write. Writing is not easy. Particularly for young children, it presents many mechanical and technical difficulties, such as letter formation, spelling, and punctuation. Moreover, writing is often taught in elementary school as a collection of formal skills rather than as a means of self-expression and communication. Emphasis on the mechanical and technical skills of writing means that, in Don Holdaway's words, "by the time most of us have left school, the pen has become the heaviest implement we will ever lift."[10] The pen may feel particularly heavy to those children who find little support for writing outside of school, and who have no reasons and purposes for writing—other than that of meeting the demands of their teacher. Helping children to find their own uses for writing is a way to give them an entry point to this complex cultural activity.

LEARNING FORMS AND FEATURES

Children must learn not only what they can do with writing but also *how* to do it—that is, they must learn about the forms and features of written language, and they must master the skills needed for writing. Although children's early experiments with writing are often related to play, at times they work very hard to master particular skills, sometimes to the point of tears and frustration. Paul Bissex, for example, at the age of 5, struggled to grasp the complexities of English spelling: "He was not playfully experimenting but focusing so earnestly on his self-set task of putting language into print that the house was at once hushed and electrified by the tension, with its triumphs and tears" (p. 11). Indeed, if left to their own devices, many children choose to spend time trying to form letters and write words, engaging in self-imposed tasks such as making lists of words they know or copying texts.

Children's efforts to master some aspect of writing often overlap with their playful and communicative uses of writing; that is, children show an interest in mastering particular skills *while* they are trying to use writing to make a sign for their bedroom door or to compose a poem or to communicate with someone by letter. Play and mastery inform and nourish each other: play is a way for children to try out what they are in the process of mastering, and to discover what they want to work on next.

Researchers have observed developmental patterns in children's early mastery of the formal aspects of writing. But there is considerable individual variation in early writing development: different children develop skills and understandings at different ages. Also, some children demonstrate different levels of writing in different contexts—they use real letters and real words on one occasion and scribble-writing on another, depending on their immediate interests and purposes. The course of writing development is not neatly linear and does not occur in fixed sequences. There are no reliable developmental milestones tied to age as there are in the course of physical growth and development; how and when writing develops depends a great deal on a child's particular circumstances. It seems likely that there is more than one route to learning to write, and that differences in how and when children learn to write are the rule, rather than the exception.[11]

Although the course of learning to write is not the same for all children, it is not a random one. It reflects children's cognitive developmental level as well as their particular experiences with written language. As Piaget has shown us, young children are active learners, constantly trying to make sense of their world. When young children learn how to write, as when they learn how to talk, they engage in active problem-solving, extracting information from their experiences, forming hypotheses, and constructing rules. These rules are tried out, revised, reconstructed, gradually coming closer to conventional forms and mature adult usage. When children live in an environment in which written language is used in interesting and meaningful ways, much of this construction process appears to take place spontaneously. As children observe others writing and reading, and as they ask questions, experiment, and participate in writing and reading activities with others, they gradually come to understand and control the formal aspects of written language.

SCRIBBLING AND SPELLING

At about the age of 18 months most children are able to hold a pencil and, if offered pencil and paper, will begin to scribble. Scribbling appears to start as a motor activity in which children explore the movements of pencils, crayons, and markers on paper. These movements leave a trace, which makes them interesting, and children soon discover that they can cover pieces of paper (and many other surfaces!) with their markings. Scribbling becomes a way of acting on the world, a way of making something that didn't exist before; this is part of the appeal of both drawing and writing.

Early scribbles often have a random, disorganized quality, reflecting the young scribbler's lack of fine motor coordination and control. As control and coordination develop, recognizable shapes and patterns—lines, dots, circles—begin to emerge, and the products begin to be labeled as drawings or as writing. There is some disagreement among researchers as to whether drawing precedes writing developmentally or whether they develop simultaneously. Most children do seem to develop control over drawing before writing; that is, they are able to produce recognizable drawings before they can produce recognizable writing.[12]

It is possible to see differences between many children's drawings and writings at an early age, and this suggests that, at times, children consciously try to imitate writing. Some young children begin to differentiate writing from drawing in their own productions almost from the time they start to scribble. Giti Baghban, whose early writing and reading activities were closely scrutinized by her mother, began to scribble at 17 months and to produce what she called "writing" at 20 months. Her mother observed that Giti "often attempted to write as soon as possible after watching an adult write," and that her writing on these occasions was more likely to resemble real writing than it did at other times.[13]

The age at which children begin to make marks on paper that they identify as writing probably depends on their experience with written language and on how their parents and siblings react to their marks on paper. Children who are exposed to writing and whose scribbling and pretend writing are responded to with interest and enthusiasm are likely to produce what they define as writing at an earlier age than children who have little exposure to writing or whose early efforts are ignored or discouraged.

From scribbles to letters. Marie Clay, a New Zealand educator and one of the pioneers in studying children's early writing, has proposed that when preschool children begin to write they incorporate features of mature or conventional writing into their own writing. That is, when children encounter writing in their environment, they notice visual features such as linearity, horizontality, and repetition (the fact that the same shapes recur again and again), and they then use this information to construct their own principles and concepts about writing. For example, the "flexibility principle" is the understanding that letters consist of a limited number of shapes that can be put together in various ways. The "generating principle" is the understanding that a small number of shapes can be used to generate a variety of letters—and, later, that a limited number of letters can generate a variety of words, and that a limited number of words can generate a great many sentences.[14]

As children learn that marks and letters represent or stand for something, they are developing an understanding of what Clay calls the "sign concept." This achievement, which is of central importance in learning to read and write, is not necessarily an all-or-nothing affair. Children may come to understand that marks on paper have some kind of meaning without necessarily understanding what that meaning is or understanding the precise nature of the relationship between signs and their meanings. Beginning writers may look for concrete relationships between marks or letters and what they stand for, sometimes apparently expecting a physical resemblance between the two. For example, they may think, as 3-year-old Santiago did, that the "word elephant must have 'many, many letters' because elephant is 'the biggest in the world.' "[15] Clay and others have noted that children often make scribbles or jumbles of letters and then ask an adult, "What did I write?"— apparently believing that the marks they have produced are readable by someone who knows how to read. On the other hand, some children may know that their writing is not really writing but choose to pretend that it is.

Clay has shown that children's early efforts at writing reflect their close attention to the written language in their environment, and their struggle to make sense of print as they use it. Support for Clay's arguments comes from other researchers who have observed that children's scribble-writing differs from culture to culture: scribbling by children who speak Arabic or Hebrew looks quite different from scribbling by English-speaking children.[16] Scribble or pretend writing is not random, meaningless behavior; rather, it is evidence of learning in progress. Clay also notes that children use writing principles and concepts without formal instruction if they are involved in meaningful experiences with written language, and if they are encouraged to scribble and write as they choose.

Rachel's letters. A child named Rachel wrote a series of letters to her grandmother. These letters provide glimpses of one child learning to use and control one particular form of writing. The first letter her mother observed was written when Rachel was 2½ years old, not long after her brother Joshua's sixth birthday. When Joshua was being urged to write thank-you letters, Rachel made a series of wavy lines on a piece of paper and told her mother it was a "thank-you letter to Grandma." About six months later, Rachel made letterlike marks on a piece of lined paper and told her mother it said "Dear Grandma and Grandpa. Thank you for the lots of presents. Love, Rachel." She then asked her mother to "get the stuff to mail it to them." A year and a half after this, when Rachel was 4½ and Joshua had recently turned 8, Rachel took a piece of her brother's lined stationery and made neat rows of letters and letterlike shapes (in no apparent order). Then she said to her mother, "I want to write a letter. I have to write a thank-you note to Grandma." She asked, "How do you spell 'Dear Grandma I love my presents'?" Her mother wrote this out for her. Rachel copied "Dear Grandma," then stopped, saying "this is boring," and asked her mother to write the rest. Her mother did, and the finished letter was mailed to her grandmother.

As Rachel's writing skills developed, she was able to manage more of the mechanics of writing herself. When she was about 5, she wrote a message to her father for Father's Day (on the back of a commercial greeting card). This time, Rachel composed the message, her mother supplied the spelling, and Rachel did all the writing herself:

EAT TOO
MUCH TICKLES
AND ONE
SCOOP OF
SPAGHETTI.

Here, Rachel was working hard to produce "real" or conventional writing, while at the same time she was taking a playful approach to its content.

The evolution in Rachel's writing from wavy lines to letterlike marks to mixtures of letters and letterlike shapes is similar to the developmental patterns identified by Clay and other researchers. Thus, when Rachel made a set of wavy lines she was demonstrating her understanding of directionality, linearity, and repetition (or in Clay's terms, the "directional principle" and the "recurring principle"). When she later made letterlike shapes, she was employing the "flexibility principle" and the "generating principle." Only the playful note to her father resembles conventional writing, but each of the letters reflects Rachel's developing understanding of what writing is, and her increasing ability to control it. This developmental progression of control and skill is similar to that of many young writers who begin to experiment with writing in supportive environments.

Rachel's writing activities were closely embedded in her relationships with family members: with her brother, her mother, her grandmother, and her father. Rachel had no literal reason to thank her grandmother at the time she wrote these letters; presumably she chose the thank-you-letter form because her brother was writing thank-you letters and she wanted to emulate him. We can also assume that she wanted to communicate with her grandmother. In using writing, Rachel was learning to take advantage of the relative permanence of written language, which makes it possible to communicate over time and space—in this case, to communicate with a grandmother who lived a thousand miles away. Rachel may also have been interested in engaging her mother's interest and support in her writing efforts. In the third letter, as happens with many young writers, Rachel's ambition outran her patience with the mechanics of writing. Because her mother was willing to serve as a scribe, Rachel was able to complete the letter. The last letter to her father was a way to communicate with him, a way to acknowledge a special occasion, and a way to demonstrate her developing competence as a writer.

As she wrote these letters, Rachel was learning about one particular form of writing; she was learning about the mechanics of writing and the process of composing a written text; and she was learning that she could *use* writing for something—in this case, to imitate her brother, to make contact with some of the important people in her life, and, in a larger sense, to participate in an activity that is valued by her family and her culture.

Invented spelling. Between the ages of 4 and 7, some children invest considerable interest and energy in trying to master the mysteries of English spelling, struggling to translate words they can say into the letters that spell them. They seem to be intrigued by the discovery that the words they speak can be broken into letters, so that figuring out what letters make up familiar words becomes an interesting and challenging puzzle. The mother of 5-year-old Stephen described his interest in spelling this way:

> He approaches it in two ways. Sometimes he is looking for straightforward information about how a word is spelled or what sound a particular letter makes. He's obviously fitting something together in his mind, and when he gets the information he wants to go off and piece it together. Other times he seems to be playing with what he already knows and deriving pleasure and a great sense of pride from his new expertise. For example, he made up a crazy knock, knock joke:

Stephen:	Knock, knock.
Mother:	Who's there?
Stephen:	Bell.
Mother:	Bell who?
Stephen:	Bell T.
Mother:	(questioning look)
Stephen:	Get it? BELT!

Paul Bissex also engaged in "mental spelling," analyzing how sounds and letters are put together to make words. On one occasion, he observed to his mother that "if you took the L out of 'glass' and pushed it all together, you'd have 'gas' "; on another, he announced, "I am N-O-T going to pick carrots" (pp. 14, 15).

Learning to spell in English is not an easy task. The relationships between the sounds of words and their spellings are often inconsistent and complex. To spell correctly, children must learn, for example, that the same letter can have different sounds, depending in part on its context (such as the "c" in "cat," "cent," or "chair"), and that the same sound can be represented with different letters (as in "cat" and "king"). They must also learn that sometimes letters are silent, serving as markers to indicate how another letter is pronounced.

When young children begin to invent their own ways of spelling, they often employ a "letter-name" strategy, breaking words into their component sounds, and then finding a letter name to represent each sound. When children spell in this way, they use no wasted or silent letters. Thus, beginning spellers often leave out vowels, particularly silent vowels, and nasal consonants like M and N, and they are likely to leave off the long-vowel markers at the end of words, writing HAT for "hate," PLA for "play," and NAM for "name."[17] This is the strategy Paul Bissex used when he wrote his first message—RUDF— for his mother. A similar strategy was at work in many of Paul's notes, signs, and labels cited earlier.

Invented spelling may look very strange to the uninitiated reader, and it is sometimes easier to interpret if it is "sounded out" by being read aloud. This is true of the following note, written by Paul a few months after he wrote "RUDF":

EFUKANOPNKAZIWILGEVUAKANOPENR
(If you can open cans, I will give you a can opener.)
   (p. 11)

When children use invented spelling, they can often read their message soon after they have finished writing it, but later they may forget what they had in mind and not be able to make sense of what they wrote. Young children's spelling is often quite fluid, and they are likely to spell the same word in different ways, even within the same text. It is as if each time they spell a word they reinvent it, perhaps using a slightly different strategy of matching sounds and letters. Paul Bissex, for example, spelled "telephone" TLEFN one day and TALAFON three days later. This suggests that inventive spellers are "not memorizing words but rather figuring out the spelling of each word, even those written previously, as a new problem" (p. 11).

A letter-name strategy is useful for beginning writers, but it is also limited because there are forty-four phonemes, or units of sound, and only twenty-six letters in the alphabet. As their knowledge of spelling develops, children gradually learn to represent more and more speech sounds in their spelling. At the beginning of first grade, 6-year-old Darryl produced the following very abbreviated sentence:

I L N GLEAD TXS
(I live in Golead, Texas.)

Two months later, he was able to represent many more sounds when he wrote:

A MAN ROB SOS THE PLES FID HIM
(A man robbed shoes. The police found him.)[18]

When children construct their own spelling rules, they engage in an active process of problem-solving. They observe, listen, extract information, construct hypotheses about how words are spelled, and try them out. They make logical, rule-governed mistakes similar to those children make when they are learning to talk; they overgeneralize the rules they are learning, sometimes misapplying or overextending them. For example, when children who are learning to talk learn to use the past tense, they are likely to add "ed" to every verb they utter, producing sentences such as "I goed" or "I runned." When children experiment with spelling, they make similar kinds of overgeneralizations. Paul Bissex used TH to spell the sounds made by "sh," "ch," and "zh," producing FENETH (finish), THANL (channel), and TARATHR (treasure) (p. 24).

Many children engage in a similar process of invention and experimentation with the rules of punctuation and capitalization. They may use dots rather than spaces to indicate word boundaries, as Paul Bissex did when he wrote these directions:

HAU.TO.DO.TH.ENDEN.WOR.DANS
FRST.U.TAK WAN.AV.UOR.FET.
(How to do the Indian war dance.
First you take one of your feet. . .) (p. 26)

On occasion, Paul also used dots to segment sounds *within* words, producing AFTR.NUN (afternoon) and TAL.A.FON. (telephone) (p. 23).

Children may encounter conflicts among their spelling strategies. For example, in response to instruction at school when he was in first grade, Paul developed a "visual" spelling strategy based on trying to remember how words *look*. For a time, this interfered with the "phonemic" strategy he had been using, which was based on how words *sound*. This conflict led to some odd misspellings of words he had previously spelled correctly, such as TIHS (this), TEH (the), and HUOSE (house). Bissex noted that these were "errors in the direction of progress" because "more mature, competent spellers of English know that a word is correct if it 'looks right' " (pp. 43–44). Eventually, Paul integrated the two strategies.

As Bissex, Ferreiro, and others suggest, the kinds of errors children make in spelling and punctuation indicate that they are paying close attention to written language—they are trying to make connections between spoken and written language and between the written language they encounter in their environment and their own writing. Carol Chomsky has suggested that inventing their own spellings may give children a sense of ownership of writing and reading because "the printed word 'belongs' to the spontaneous speller in a way in which it cannot, at least at the start, belong to children who have experienced it only ready-made."[19] Not all children are willing to use invented spelling, however. Some children seem to know that there is only one right way to spell most words, and from the beginning insist on spelling correctly, refusing to write anything unless they are sure of the conventional spelling.

Writing names.   Not surprisingly, the first word many children learn to spell correctly is their given name. Children encounter their name in writing again and again, at home and in preschool and kindergarten. They often begin by learning the first letter of their name, which they often refer to as "my letter" or sometimes as "my name," and which for a time they may consider to *be* their name.[20] In recording kindergarten children's comments about written language, Dyson noted the central importance children gave to their own names:

Child's Talk	*Graphics*
Courtney: "That's part of Vivi's name."	V
Mark: "That's the same as I am!"	A
Marcos: "That's *not* my name [i.e., even though there's an A, and a C, it's not my name].	BAC
Rachel: "This [B] goes in Brian's name. This [l] goes in my name. This [r] goes in my name. This [i] goes in Brian's name."[21]	Blri

In learning to recognize and write their own names, children are acquiring useful information about written language. When they learn the letters that make up their names, they are learning that an "invariant set of letters and order of letters . . . make up a remembered word." Moreover, the name "becomes a repository of known letters" that the child can use to recognize and produce other words.[22] Children also see that their names can be written in various ways: for example, entirely in capitals or with an initial capital followed by lowercase letters, and with slight variations in letter formation depending on the handwriting of the writer. Thus children can begin to distinguish the essential, enduring features of print from irrelevant variations in form.

Writing stories. Here is the first story written by 6-year-old Karla, a child in the after-school program described earlier:

> The little Deborah
> Onec apon a time there lived a Gril named
> Deborah. She was in a Plane hihn in sky.
> She a very good Gril. She was very
> nice to her parents and she liked to
> Play Barbies wihe her friends.
> The End.

This simple text represents a considerable achievement. In constructing an imaginative narrative about Deborah (one of the group workers in the program), Karla put together her knowledge of spelling and punctuation, story plots, and literary language, as well as her experience with fantasy and pretend play. She used both conventional and invented spelling, as well as her knowledge of literary structure, language, and conventions. She gave her story an appropriate title, and opened with a typical storybook beginning, "Onec apon a time." She continued with language clearly acquired from experience with books, "there lived a Gril named Deborah," and she closed with a conventional ending, "The End."

Karla's peers also engaged in playful explorations of literary forms and conventions they had encountered in their reading. One 6-year-old girl wrote a page of titles, then a page of story beginnings, then a page of story endings. Many children wrote stories that began with "once upon a time" and ended with "they lived happily ever after," and some children played with being different speakers and using different voices, writing sentences such as "oh no she cryd" and "then she said 'oh, my donkey is missing.' "

When Karla wrote "The little Deborah," she also drew on her experience with play. As in dramatic pretend play, she created an imaginary situation, here imagining someone else's experience in another time and place. She also engaged in a kind of role-play with Deborah, making the group worker—a large and powerful figure in her world—into a little girl who likes to do the same kinds of things that she, Karla, does. Thus, Karla did with writing what children so often do in pretend play when they reverse everyday role and power relationships and subject important adult figures to their imaginative control. (This is akin to what Maria did when she wrote the tests and challenges for her "techers" described earlier.)

In writing their own stories, children may be trying to recreate the kind of imaginative experience they know from fantasy and pretend play, and from reading and being read to. Jerome Bruner has suggested that "what initially attracts children to reading and into mastering all the mechanics of it is the opportunity that text provides for penetrating possible worlds, worlds beyond the mundanities of here and now."[23] It seems likely that children are attracted to writing for the same reason. By composing their own texts, they create opportunities for entering "possible worlds."

LEARNING WRITING PROCESSES

As mature writers know, the process of composing and constructing a written text is anything but simple. Linda Flower and John Hayes studied adults as they wrote and concluded that "a writer caught in the act looks . . . like a very busy switchboard operator trying to juggle a number of demands on her attention and constraints on what she can do." In discussing how school-age children "cope with the cognitive demands of writing," Marlene Scardamalia quoted Peter Elbow: "the proposition that it is theoretically impossible to learn to write has the ring of truth." In Scardamalia's own words, "To pay conscious attention to handwriting, spelling, punctuation, word choice, syntax, textual connections, purpose, organization, clarity, rhythm, euphony, and reader characteristics would seemingly overload the information processing capacity of the best intellects."[24]

Given these daunting cognitive and literary complexities, how do young children manage to write anything at all? How can we reconcile the image of the writer as switchboard operator with the prolific output of young writers like Paul, Rachel, Joshua, Karla, Maria, Rosa, and Kevin? There seem to be two answers to these questions. First of all, young children are not aware of many of the complexities faced by more mature writers, and thus they write using what they know and ignore or work around what they don't know. Second, when young children run into difficulties and uncertainties with writing, they can ask for help from more expert writers.

SIMPLIFYING THE PROCESS

When children begin to write, they write with whatever skills they have, finding various ways to simplify the process for themselves. They form letters and spell words as best they can; they may use pretend writing; they may work around the hazards of spelling in English by inventing their own; they may produce very short texts that are surrounded and supported by talk, drawing, or play. They may use talk and drawing to plan and sustain the process of writing, and to help convey the meanings of their written texts. They also draw on their pretend play and on their reading—what they have read and what has been read to them—as Karla did when she composed "The little Deborah." Thus, children's experiences with talking, playing, drawing, and reading can serve as resources when they begin to compose their own texts.

Preschool children sometimes use talk to make a random string of letters into a text by pretending to read it aloud. Somewhat older children may use talk to rehearse or plan their writing and to guide and maintain the writing process, telling themselves and the people around them what they are writing about, and commenting on their progress. Dyson reported that 6-year-old Manuel, a meticulous and thoughtful young writer, made comments like this while he was writing: "I think that sounds good. A real little adventure story." Children may also use talk to pull others into the writing process with them, either as collaborators or as audience. Indeed, when groups of young children are engaged in the process of writing there is likely to be a great deal of lively talk.[25]

For some children, drawing "serves as a rehearsal for the text as well as an important bridge from speech to print."[26] We saw earlier that when 6-year-old Jose composed his first story ("They were walking down the road"), he relied heavily on drawing to convey his meaning. For Jose, drawing was at least as important as words in telling his story, and it also allowed him to tell a more complete story than he could have managed had he relied on writing alone. Dyson reported on another 6-year-old, Jake, who drew elaborate "action filled" pictures which he then referred to as he composed his texts—as he put it, "I copy offa the picture." While drawing can facilitate and support early writing, it may also constrain it; Jake's early stories were closely tied to his drawings, and, as a result, they "were stuck in time. In his struggle with encoding, he lost the elaborate language and extended plots [of his talk and his pretend play]. His texts described his pictures." When Jake developed more control of his writing, he "broke free of the static time frame of his pictures."[27]

Beginning writers may or may not engage in planning before they begin to write. Manuel, unlike Jake, planned his stories while he wrote, and he commented, "I don't write about my pictures. I just write stories." Some children appear to start writing without prior planning, taking their ideas from the people and objects in their immediate surroundings. Sometimes the child may simply write for the sake of writing, for the sake of putting words on paper. And even when children do plan before they write, their plans may be forgotten or abandoned in the struggle with mechanical and technical difficulties; moreover, the slowness of the writing process may make it difficult for beginners to keep track of their plans. Some children use a simple strategy to keep track of their writing, rereading the sentence they are composing from the beginning every time they add a new word.[28]

Children may simplify the writing process by completing their written texts without trying to review or revise them. Indeed, young children often seem to have considerable difficulty with revision, and at times appear to be trapped by the words they have put down on paper, unable to overcome "the saliency of their own texts" and to imagine any other way of expressing what they want to say.[29]

As children develop more competence with the mechanics of handwriting and spelling, they are likely to pay more attention to conventions such as punctuation and capitalization; as these skills develop, young writers are freer to take a greater interest in presenting interesting topics in interesting ways, and, eventually, to revise their texts. As Donald Graves noted, children who write "keep changing the problems they solve, as well as their consciousness of what they do when they write." As children develop increasing competence, they lose their innocence as writers, becoming increasingly aware of new difficulties and complexities, as well as possibilities, that earlier were hidden from their view. They come to expect more of their writing and try to do more with it. This means that as writing gets easier, it also gets harder—the task becomes more complex and more difficult.[30]

WRITING WITH ASSISTANCE

When beginning writers get help from more competent writers they can accomplish things with writing without having to cope with more complexities than they can manage at the moment. At the same time, they can begin to confront and deal with these complexities. In writing with assistance from others, children begin to learn what the process of writing is and how they can use and control it. Collaboration begins when children bring their writing (or their interest in writing) to other people, to get a response to something they have written, or to seek information or help with something they are trying to write—or when someone invites a child to collaborate in a writing project. Collaboration can begin at any point in the writing process, as novice writers seek help with planning, with mechanical and technical problems that arise in the course of trying to get ideas on paper, and with matters of style or clarity that become apparent in reviewing and revising.

Help can come in many forms, and on many levels. It may be given spontaneously and intuitively by a parent, or it may come as part of a carefully structured school writing program. The help children receive varies with their competence and knowledge. We saw earlier, for example, that as Rachel's writing skills developed, the nature of the assistance she asked for (and received) from her mother changed. Collaboration can identify many of the complexities in the writing process that may not be visible to the beginning writer, by making them overt and explicit; at the same time, it can allow the more mature writer to point out alternatives and solutions to the child. The collaboration changes, becoming more sophisticated, as the young writer develops increasing control of the writing process.

Adults can organize situations that both demonstrate the writing process to children and get the children involved in it. Some preschool and elementary school teachers, for example, have children dictate stories while the teacher writes them down (see Chapter 6). By serving as scribes and friendly editors, teachers can help children generate and organize ideas for their stories; help translate ideas into written texts by writing down the children's words; help with reviewing, by rereading parts of the text to remind authors of their story lines, by asking questions about confusions and omissions in the plot, and by reading the stories aloud to give the authors a chance to make final revisions. When adults serve as scribes and editors, they are both demonstrating and managing the complexities of the composing process for the child—and they are bringing the child into the process as an active participant.

Donald Graves and his colleagues have developed a collaborative approach to the teaching of writing in elementary school.[31] Teachers implementing Graves's approach emphasize writing as a process as well as a product; from the beginning (in kindergarten or first grade), children learn that writing can be changed—that a piece of writing can be revised, reworked, developed, and improved, to make it express what they want to say more effectively. This approach departs from more traditional writing instruction, in which the child is usually told to write something (typically, a list of words or sentences), which is then corrected for handwriting, spelling, and grammar, graded—and forgotten. Teachers using a traditional, product-oriented approach tend to focus on the formal mechanical and technical aspects of writing while paying little attention to the individual writer's communicative purposes. Thus with this approach there is a danger that, for many children, writing will become an exercise in formal mechanics divorced from personal content and intentions.

For many young children, then, writing begins as an intensely social process. As writers mature, writing becomes an increasingly solitary pursuit—but even mature writers, including adults, often seek collaboration by circulating their writing-in-progress to friends and colleagues, asking for comments and criticisms, using their friends as audiences and editors. Children are likely to alternate between writing alone and writing collaboratively with adults, siblings, and friends throughout the preschool and elementary school years, and perhaps beyond.

To develop as writers, children need to find a balance between "doing it myself" and asking for help. Young children need aid from more competent writers in order to master the complexities of the writing process, but they also need room to find their own voice in writing. It is important for adults to respect individual differences in the resources and personal styles children bring to the writing process, as well as children's need for a sense of control of the texts they produce. This means trying to be helpful but helping with a light touch; as Anne Dyson puts it, "We want to guide but not smother the emerging voices of our students."[32]

4/ Reading

Most experts agree that reading is more than a matter of identifying letters, sounds, and words; it is a process of using these skills to derive meaning from print. This process of communicating and interpreting meaning through print can begin early, long before children can read independently.

Mrs. Naylor, a preschool teacher, reads a storybook to her class of 4-year-olds at the end of each school day. A favorite book is *Mr. Gumpy's Outing* by John Burningham. Mr. Gumpy is a friendly English gentleman who goes rowing down a river on a warm summer afternoon. Neighborhood children and animals ask him if they can come with him. As he welcomes them, Mr. Gumpy reminds them not to squabble, bleat, hop about, or tease. The boat goes along merrily until the passengers begin doing just what they should not—they flap, chase, and kick; the boat tips and they all fall into the river. They swim ashore to dry off in the sun. Noticing that it is teatime, Mr. Gumpy matter-of-factly tells his friends that they will cross the fields to his house for tea. They have a splendid tea with fruit, sandwiches, and cakes. Mr. Gumpy then bids his friends goodbye and invites them to come for a ride another day.

Mrs. Naylor thinks of this story as a metaphor for

teachers and children in school. The ideal teacher is much like Mr. Gumpy, a kind and responsible adult who welcomes children to come along on an outing. Teachers give children reminders about not chasing, kicking, and squabbling, and children usually comply, but there are days when they forget how to control their strong feelings. At such times, Mrs. Naylor strives to maintain her composure as Mr. Gumpy does, and to help the group regain good feelings before going home, so that the children will look forward to coming for an outing with her another day.

One day in class an incident suggested that the children found a similar meaning in the story of Mr. Gumpy. As the children scrambled to get their coats and line up to go outside at the end of the day, several began to shove, trying to be first in line. Willie, who had actually arrived first, was pushed out of the way. He looked back at the group for a minute, and then quietly walked to the end of the line. Jason, who had pushed him, after a moment of stunned surprise called out, "Hey, he's Mr. Gumpy!" The teacher and children broke into laughter, and the teacher said, "Willie *is* like Mr. Gumpy. Thanks for letting Jason be first, Willie."

Here a story from a book helps Jason interpret a friend's surprising behavior. Usually children fight back to preserve their place in line—but the story of Mr. Gumpy opens up new possibilities for how people can react. These children, not yet able to read for themselves, are already using reading as a means of interpreting their world. The people, places, and ideas that Mrs. Naylor's children encounter in books bring new meanings to their everyday experiences, and offer them new insights into their own feelings and ideas and those of others.

Like writing, reading requires such sophisticated

mental processes that it seems remarkable that children learn to read by the time they are 5 to 8 years old.

> Reading can be compared to the performance of a symphony orchestra. This analogy illustrates three points. First, like the performance of a symphony, reading is a holistic act. In other words, while reading can be analyzed into subskills such as discriminating letters and identifying words, performing the subskills one at a time does not constitute reading. Reading can be said to take place only when the parts are put together in a smooth, integrated performance. Second, success in reading comes from practice over long periods of time, like skill in playing musical instruments. Indeed, it is a lifelong endeavor. Third, as with a musical score, there may be more than one interpretation of a text. The interpretation depends upon the background of the reader, the purpose for reading, and the context in which reading occurs.[1]

Reading a telephone message, a newspaper, a letter, or a novel, then, involves complex psychological processes that we are rarely conscious of. When people read, they coordinate the flow of their own thinking with that of an author removed from them in time and space. The meaning that is taken from a text adds to the reader's current thinking, and may transform previous ideas and past experiences. But all of this can take place only after the reader masters a complex symbol system twice removed from the object or idea being discussed: print is a symbol for spoken words, which in turn are symbols for objects, experiences, and ideas.

Glenda Bissex describes beginning reading as a "passage from language heard to language seen."[2] It is hard for most adults to remember making the transition from speaking and listening to reading. Even when observing or teaching young children it is difficult to see what they are doing and learning: reading is a less visible and more internal activity than writing. Listening to children reading aloud and discussing something they have read are ways that adults can learn about the workings of children's minds when they read. In addition, breakdowns in learning to read provide opportunities to study the process of reading more closely, as specialists do when they try to understand the children's difficulties.

Susan Kontos has pointed out that "before they can become readers, young children must learn *why* people read and what people *do* when they read."[3] As in learning about writing, young children begin to understand the enterprise of reading from observing and participating in activities with family members and other more competent readers. When young children see other people reading, and when others read to them or involve them in other activities related to reading, they become familiar with print and some of its uses. For example, when they see people who are important to them reading a recipe to bake a cake, reading the newspaper to find out what movies are on TV, or reading ads for shopping specials in local stores, young children experience reading as a meaningful activity and a part of everyday life.

The process of communication between author and reader through written language requires imagining, evaluating, reasoning, and problem-solving. According to William Gray, readers go through four mental steps in order to derive meaning from printed symbols: (1) perceiving—being able to recognize and identify individual words; (2) comprehending—finding meaning in individual words and in the ideas they convey in a particular context; (3) reacting—responding to and judging an author's message in a personal way; and

(4) integrating—assimilating the author's ideas into one's personal background and experience.[4]

Young children like those in Mrs. Naylor's preschool class can become quite proficient in three of these four steps: they become familiar with the idea that written language makes sense, that it contains ideas that have meaning for the reader; they learn to respond and react to written messages; and experiences involving written messages become part of their background knowledge, whether it be remembering a good story that was read to them or treasuring a letter from a grandparent. What remains is Gray's step one, perceiving: children must learn the particulars of the written symbol system.

LEARNING ABOUT READING

Children learn about reading and learn how to read from encountering print in their environment and from participating in reading activities with more competent readers. Adults often point out print to children and help them notice a particular configuration of letters such as the spelling of their name or road signs indicating the city where they live. The TV program *Sesame Street* highlights words, letters, and their sounds. Children also learn a great deal about print, as well as about the process of reading, from having books read to them. From these various experiences children learn about reading as a process of communication and as a process of interpreting the world. Many children also begin to learn to "break the code."

READING IN EVERYDAY ACTIVITIES

Children growing up in the United States often learn to read labels, signs, and other kinds of print they see around them. Their "sight vocabulary" might include

"STOP," "Crest" (the toothpaste), "McDonald's," names of cereals and other foods, and names of favorite books or TV shows. Print is highly visible on objects in the home, on signs, buildings, billboards, and cars, and on TV. In these cases the print often has a particular format, such as the typeface associated with the brand name Coca Cola. The print appears in a fixed context (here, on a particular type of bottle or can); it may appear in certain colors and have an accompanying design or logo; and it usually shows up in predictable types of situations (for example, Coca Cola is found on picnics, in grocery stores, in the refrigerator).

Adults and older children are likely to refer to print and its meaning in various contexts: for example, while handling objects such as packaged food or household products, looking for signs on the highway, or figuring out instructions to a game or a toy. When print is mentioned in these ways, the mention is often accompanied by some action or spoken words that indicate the meaning of the print.[5] Thus, aided by visual memory, children learn to recognize print in a particular context: where it appears, with whom, and for what purpose.

In Trackton, a southern black working-class community studied by Shirley Brice Heath, children aged 4 to 6 learn to read a variety of materials while playing, running errands for family members, helping people find their way around the community, and playing games. Preschool children begin to read the name brands of cars, motorcycles, bicycles, street signs, the names of railroad lines on passing trains, advertisements for taxi companies and other products, names of food items and their prices, and names and addresses on people's mail. By school age, many children have figured out how to read instructions for games, parts of brochures describing the use of tools, or notices of special programs to be held at church or school.[6]

Trackton children learn to read by watching others read and write for a variety of practical purposes, from participating in activities that involve reading, and sometimes from being corrected when they make mistakes. Occasionally, older children or adults give help when younger children ask for it, but adults in this community are usually not directly involved in their children's learning to read. In Trackton, learning to talk, to read, and to write are not thought of as achievements that require special adult attention or "teaching" outside of school. Literacy, like oral language development, emerges as children participate in community activities that include print.

The experience of Trackton children is similar to that of many other children during their preschool and early school years. Learning about reading in this way is gradual and incidental, since the focus of attention is usually not on print or reading itself but on an activity that involves print in some way, such as shopping for groceries. These everyday experiences do not by themselves make most children fluent readers, but they help children become familiar with print and with the process of reading for communication.

READING TO CHILDREN

Reading books to young children is a powerful way of introducing them to literacy, and it is the one early experience that has been identified as making a difference in later success in learning to read in school. But these are not usually the reasons that adults, particularly parents, read to young children. More often they do it because they find it enjoyable, they see that the child enjoys it, and they also may believe that reading nourishes children's minds and imaginations and enriches their relationships. When adults read to children, the occasion tends to be warm and intimate; parents, caretakers, or older children often hold young children on their laps or sit close to them while reading aloud, and their attention is focused on the interaction with the child. The reader is usually sensitive to what interests the children, what scares them, what they are curious about, and what delights them. Reading often includes conversations about the characters in the book, about what they might be thinking and feeling, and about experiences in the child's own life that are related to those in the book.

The activity of storybook reading, particularly of mothers' reading to infants and toddlers, has been the subject of several studies during the past ten years (most of them focused on white middle-class mothers and children). These studies show that early reading of picture books is likely to be a social, collaborative process; interactions tend to be conversational and often are both playful or game-like and instructional. Parents sometimes begin reading to children as young as 6 months old, often choosing picture books without words or a story line. Most parents do not just show the pictures to children but instead talk about them, asking questions like "What's that?" or making comments like "That's a lion. Remember when we saw the lion at the zoo?"

When children are read to from an early age, they are, according to Catherine Snow and Anat Ninio, "inducted into the contracts of literacy." These contracts are the rules that govern routines for "the use of books as communicative partners. Very few of the rules of literacy are explicit or can be taught explicitly. Reading and comprehending texts depend on many tacit 'contracts' and 'metacontracts' . . . between literate persons concerning the use of books and the meaning of texts—contracts which have very little to do with the ability to decipher a written word."[7]

Snow and Ninio describe some of the contracts that children come to understand implicitly from picture-book reading:

1. "Books are for reading, not for manipulating." Books are not to be treated as toys or as food. Children discover that books belong to a category of "objects of contemplation" as opposed to objects of action.[8]

2. "In book reading, the book is in control; the reader is led." The pictures and words of the text determine what readers think about and discuss.

3. "Pictures are not things but representatives of things." What is on the pages of a book is a *symbol* and needs to be interpreted and treated as such; children learn not to try to eat a pictured ice-cream cone or listen to a picture of a fire engine.

4. "Pictures are for naming." When young children learn to name the pictures in books, they are learning that books elicit words; later they will transfer this notion to print: they will understand that print elicits words from the reader.

5. "Pictures, though static, can represent events." When children participate in reading books, they learn that pictures (and print) can represent far more than an object or a person; they can represent feelings, motives, relationships, and sequences of events. Children learn to build an active, lively, coherent world for storybook characters and events.

6. "Book events occur outside of real time."

7. "Books constitute an autonomous fictional world." Children learn that fictional characters live in a time and place separate from and independent of a child's own

world. Moreover, they learn that they can use books to return to their favorite fictional worlds again and again.

The interactions between parents and young children in early reading of picture books are likely to be highly repetitive routines.[9] Parents tend to organize book reading with predictable kinds of utterances. They get their child's attention by pointing to a picture and saying "Look." Next they ask "What's that?" Often they answer their own question by supplying the label for the picture, and if the child makes gestures and vocalizations, the parent may add a confirmation: "That's right. It is a _____ ." This pattern of dialogue is repeated page after page, with parents carrying out as many of the conversational moves as necessary; in the beginning, the infant may contribute nothing more than visual attention.

The format changes over time. As soon as parents recognize a vocalization from their child that is a close approximation to the actual label for a picture, they change their response. In Jerome Bruner's phrase, they "raise the ante"; they withhold the label and repeat the query until the child vocalizes; then they give the label as they confirm the child's utterance: "Yes, it is a _____ ." Parents keep their children performing at the highest level they are capable of by continually increasing the demands they make of their children, but all the while making sure the children are successful in responding to their questions. Through these remarkable intuitive strategies, parents organize a progressively more complex learning situation for a child—one that is finely tuned to the child's needs, and one that remains within the context of playful and conversationally appropriate interchanges between parent and child.[10]

Judith Lindfors provides a close look at this type of

picture-book reading between a mother (M) and her
14-month-old child, Sarah (C):

1. M: What's this?
2. C: bah
3. M: Ball. Good girl. What's this?
4. C: yah
5. M: Car.
6. C: gah
7. M: Clock. Good girl. Tick-tock, tick-tock, tick-tock.
8. C: naah
9. M: Wha—
10. C: nnah
11. M: What's this?
12. C: nah
13. M: Chair.
14. C: beebee
15. M: Blocks.
16. C: bee
17. M: You have blocks. You see. Uh-hm. What's
    this?
18. C: lahyah
19. M: Flo-wer.
20. C: ihgee
21. M: What's this?
22. C: weebah
23. M: Boat.
24. C: uhbeeguhwuduhwuduhwuduhbah
25. M: Book.
26. C: yah yah
27. M: Flowers. Good girl.
28. C: yah-ee
29. M: Yes.[11]

This dialogue follows the kind of routinized pattern described earlier. Lindfors points out that in this conversation the mother and child construct a "text" as they

progress through the book—a "story" that consists of one word per picture. Their dialogue shows sensitivity on both their parts: mother and child pay close attention to each other, shaping their comments in response to each other and taking alternate turns to speak.

Occasionally Sarah's mother helps her make connections between the book and other experiences in her life by giving more information than just the label of a picture (lines 7 and 17). Such comments are frequent when mothers read to young children, and are usually brief references to more general aspects of the child's past experience rather than to specific events. Such information helps children "use their knowledge of the world to make sense of the text."[12]

By the time Sarah was 16 months old, the mother-child reading had changed from conversational naming of pictures to "following fictional characters in an action sequence." Sarah's mother would weave aspects of literary narrative into the conversation, and Sarah would respond to and sometimes extend these ideas, thereby contributing to the reading process. The following conversation took place while mother and daughter were looking at one of Sarah's favorite picture books, *Snow White*.

1. C: e-e-e
2. M: The wicked old witch says, "Yeh-heh-heh."
3. C: weee
4. M: Where's that wicked old witch?
5. C: yeee (whimper)
6. M: It's not a *page*. It's not a *page*, it's the cover.
7. C: bee eh-he-eeee
8. M: That's what she *says*. "Yeh-he-he. Have an apple, deary." There, she gives Snow White an apple and Snow White takes *one* bite and *falls*

asleep forever, until Prince Charming comes.
One bite of apple. (lip smacking) Is it good?

9. C: nah wah wah (lip smacking)
10. M: What is this? What is this? (lip smacking)
    What's Momma eating? Apple? Ummmmmm
    good.
11. C: uhwuhwuh
12. M: Those birds.
13. C: gih
14. M: What does bird say?
15. C: eegee
16. M: Tweet, tweet, tweet. We hear 'em in the
    morning.
17. C: gee
18. M: Uh-hm. Mmmmm, do you take a bite of that
    apple? Is it good?
19. C: (lip smacking sounds)
20. M: Mmm yum yum. (p. 10)

For Sarah and her mother, the making of meaning is central to the activity of reading a book. Sarah's mother carries the major responsibility for organizing and shaping her child's responses into a meaningful flow of ideas. The child's learning about the reading of books and the telling of stories is embedded in the interaction with her mother—in their mutual interest in finding meaning in each other's gestures and words.

Being read to initiates children into the world of books and reading in subtle ways. In William Teale's phrase, the child's learning takes place as "fallout" from the interaction between parent and child, an inevitable outcome of a satisfying interpersonal experience in which stories and pictures capture the interest and imagination of both child and adult.[13] Parents keep children involved in books by asking them questions, having them identify people and objects, having them turn the pages of the book, making comments, and using a voice intonation appropriate to reading books and to the particular story. Thus each session of picture-book reading offers children a lesson in the "contracts of literacy."

Children take great pleasure in being read to; this is clear from the frequency and persistence with which they ask adults to read to them. Some children do this nonverbally: Marcia Baghban described how her daughter Giti, a toddler who loved to be read to, often "chose a book, stood in front of someone she decided could read, and backed up to the reader."[14] Our experience with 2-to-4-year-old children who have *not* been read to regularly suggests that it does not take long for children to get hooked on the experience. We observed this when regular storybook reading was introduced to Head Start classrooms for the first time; teachers quickly discovered that 3- and 4-year-olds loved to listen to stories, provided that books were carefully selected and read well. We observed a similar process when a small number of low-income black and Hispanic mothers of children in a Head Start program began reading to their children at home. These mothers soon found their children demanding to be read to, and found themselves struggling to find the time to read to them once a day. It seems that children can be introduced to books at various ages, and that they can develop strong, positive feelings about books and being read to, especially when the reading is embedded in relationships with people who are important to them.

Many educators and anthropologists have emphasized the importance of reading to young children because of its contribution to the development of a "literacy orientation," a "literacy set," or "emergent literacy."[15] Children who enjoy being read to are in a prime position to acquire a wide range of knowledge about written language and about the process of reading. Being read to shows children that writing comes in a variety of forms, such as stories and poems. Print— the little black squiggles or marks on the page—is a courier; children gradually learn that reading involves getting the information and the author's meaning from these marks on the page. Children come to understand that the reader is not free-associating to pictures or graphics but rather is reconstructing a story through the printed words that were set down by an author. As children acquire favorite storybooks, they learn that print makes language permanent; the words in books always stay the same whether the book is being read at home, in school, or at a friend's house. Books can be read and reread, they can be closed, carried to distant places, and opened again, but the words remain the same!

Children also learn that the language of storybooks is different from the language they use in daily conversations. Written language has its own rhythms and cadences. For example, children learn to expect storybooks to begin with literary conventions such as "Once upon a time there lived an old man near the deep blue sea," and to end with phrases such as "and he lived happily ever after." They also come to expect and enjoy literary language such as "One day he said to his son, 'Let us go into the forest and search for the tallest oak tree.' " As they are read to, children begin to pay close attention to language itself; this becomes evident when they object to a reader's attempts to change the words in a favorite book, and when they incorporate storybook language into their fantasy and pretend play.

Being read to exposes children to new words and new uses of familiar words. For example, in the story *The Three Billy Goats Gruff*, children hear words such as "meadow," "trample," and "hooves," which they are not likely to encounter in everyday conversation. Most often, children evolve an understanding of such words from the pictures and the parts of the story that they do understand. Associating new words with a story they love helps children to remember them and to develop an understanding of their meaning.

As children are read to, they learn that words can create a world of experience, that words can build a context for thinking and talking that is removed from the immediate here and now. From listening to storybooks, children learn to let their attention and thinking be guided by words, rather than relying on objects and people around them to establish the topic of conversation and the intended meanings of words. Listening to stories gives children practice in the kind of experience they will have when they read independently, when they will have to rely on a written text to construct ideas that carry meaning. In Bruner's words, when reading a text, "you cannot 'read the situation' to figure out what the message might mean as you can easily do in most face-to-face conversation. The context of a written text is more text."[16]

As children listen to stories being told or read aloud, and as they discuss them with others, they acquire an understanding of narrative structure, an intuitive sense of what a story is. They learn that stories have a beginning, a middle, and an end, and that there is some problem or conflict that is described and then resolved. They become accustomed to different kinds of fictional characters—such as villains and heroes—and they learn about the motivations of various types of people in various predicaments.

What children learn from being read to can play an important role when they go to school and begin formal instruction in reading and writing. And it is not only before school age that reading to children is important. Kindergarten children (in Israel) whose teachers read to them in school three times a week for four months were better able to understand stories and to make inferences about causal relationships; were more attentive to picture cues; and could construct better narratives than a matched control group who were not read to. First-grade children whose teachers read to them daily for twenty minutes over a six-month period had higher comprehension scores, used more complex language in storytelling, and made fewer errors in their own oral reading than a matched control group who were not read to.[17] These findings suggest that regardless of what reading is going on at home, reading to children in school helps them learn to read—and to interpret—for themselves.

Whether at home or in child-care or school settings, reading books to children is a way of using written language to create shared experiences in thinking about ideas, and a way of making connections between children's personal worlds and the larger group they are a part of—be it their family, their classmates, or a neighborhood group of friends. It also is a way to give children an appetite for stories, and therefore for reading. Children learn that storybooks bring them special pleasures that cannot be gotten in any other way. Their delight in what books have to offer can become one of their main sources of motivation for learning the more technical aspects of decoding print—which is necessary for learning to read.

PLAYING WITH READING

Young children who are read to often introduce reading into their fantasy play—they may pretend to read books to dolls or stuffed animals, or they may incorporate written materials into their play as Joshua did when he "read" the ABC News (see Chapter 2). In their early explorations of the activity of reading, children begin to make sense of reading, to learn about it as a process of communication, and to understand how it can help them interpret the world in new ways.

Books can be a rich source of plots, characters, and elaborate language, along with ideas and fantasies, which children use to create their own stories and to nurture their pretend play. Playing with story ideas can begin very early. Lindfors describes how Sarah, at 19 months old, pulled her mother into a reenactment of *Snow White*. One day when Sarah was finishing her lunch, her mother asked "Are you all done?" Sarah responded with a line from the story, this time with no book or props present.

1. C: Ha hooooo heh
2. M: "Hi ho, hi ho, it's off to work we go." (sung)
3. C: (blowing attempt at whistling)
4. M: (whistles next line of song) "Hi ho. . ." (sung)
5. C: miomiomiowaw
6. M: "Mirror, mirror on the wall, who's the fairest of them all?"
7. C: owahwiawwuhmioowahmioowah
8. M: "Mirror, mirror on the wall," the wicked old queen says that in *Snow White*. "Mirror, mirror on the wall."
9. C: eh-eh-eh-eh
10. M: "Eh-eh-eh. Would you like an apple, deary?"
11. C: abaw
12. M: She takes an apple. Snow White takes an apple.
13. C: uh-oh
14. M: What happens when Snow White takes an apple? Then what happens? What happens

with Snow White? She *takes* an apple and *falls* asleep forever.
15. C: oh dish ("kiss")
16. M: Uh-hm. And then the prince comes and gives her a kiss. Yeah. And he comes on his white horse.
17. C: boobabit
18. M: Huh?
19. C: uhbabit ahbabit
20. M: A blanket? He brings her a blanket? The prince? No.   (p. 11)

Sarah is thinking about one of her favorite storybooks, and she gets her mother to help her play out some of the story's events by retelling them. Lindfors points out that although Sarah's utterances are limited to one or two words, she uses these resources to convey the story as best she can. Because of the finely tuned conversational partnership between parent and child, Sarah's mother can fill in the details, providing the words her daughter cannot yet produce. What is striking is that Sarah's "sense of the story narrative, her recognition of and adherence to text, is unmistakable" (p. 5). Thus, long before she is able to talk fluently, Sarah understands how to participate in telling a story.

One afternoon, a grandmother watched her 2½-year-old granddaughter, Jennifer, in solitary pretend play. Jennifer acted out a scene from a storybook her parents had been reading to her, Kipling's *Jungle Book*. Jennifer was sitting under a large hydrangea bush in the backyard with a long stick in her hand and said, "Mowgli is my friend." Then she waved the stick around and said, "Go away, Shere Khan, go into the woods." She repeated this several times, and then announced loudly, "Shere Kahn has gone into the woods." When adults read a book that they find interesting or moving in some way, they are likely to talk about it with family or friends. Young children, like Jennifer, often reflect on situations in storybooks, savor their memories, and deepen their understanding of them in fantasy play.

When he was 4 years old, in his bath Joshua would tell himself long stories of hardship and rescue, which included sentences in literary language such as "all but one has fled," "they all ran away save one who stayed," and "Goodbye, he said, stepping into his boat." Joyce Carol Oates, in discussing her own development as a writer, said that she discovered at the age of 3 or 4 that "telling stories . . . is a way of being told stories."[18] For children, using literary characters, plots, and language to tell or retell themselves stories may serve as a bridge to reading. In playing with storybook characters and reenacting scenes from books in literary language, children try out the voice of a reader—thus first experiencing reading in the context of play.

Sarah, Jennifer, and Joshua are comfortable with moving back and forth between seeing themselves in the possible worlds of play and stories and seeing themselves in the world of their everyday life. Being able to shift back and forth between the immediate here-and-now and the possible worlds of storybooks gives children new ways to interpret their world. They begin to see a relationship between the real and the possible, and their understanding of one can nurture their understanding of the other. This happened for Jason in Mrs. Naylor's class when he watched his friend Willie so calmly give up his place in line; it reminded him of Mr. Gumpy's calm way of managing a whole group of disruptive passengers by inviting them all to tea.

Another way children play at reading and practice the

voice of a reader is by pretending to read storybooks by themselves. Don Holdaway was probably the first to point out that very young children who are frequently read to spend a great deal of time on their own with their favorite storybooks, pretending to read them and reenacting the behaviors they observed while they were being read to. Young children's independent efforts to read books demonstrate the wealth of knowledge about books, print, and narratives they acquire while they are being read to. In observing a number of children between the ages of 2 and 5 "reading" favorite storybooks, Holdaway was struck by how hard the children worked to recapture the meaning of stories: "They have remembered very little at the surface verbal level; what they have remembered most firmly is meanings."[19] The children were not giving a memorized rendition of a story, but were, instead, working to reconstruct the message of the story using the rhythms and sounds of language in which they had first heard that message.

Elizabeth Sulzby describes a progression of changes in children's pretend reading as they gradually approach independent reading. Preschoolers' reading of favorite books is, for the most part, guided by "reading" the pictures in the book. Young children hold the book and turn the pages quite deliberately, while naming or commenting on what they see in the pictures. In time, and as they become more familiar with the story, they "read" the book by making up a story, creating a rough story line that follows the sequence of pictures. Gradually the language they use in "reading" (while still looking at the pictures), sounds more and more like real reading—the child's voice and intonation come to sound like written language read aloud.[20]

Children at ages 3, 4, or 5 may give close renditions or

even verbatim recitations of stories they have heard frequently. As Sulzby and Holdaway have observed, children do not simply memorize the text but work from a strong sense of what the "reading" of the story should sound like, and work hard to retrieve and reconstruct the text. Children strive to get the exact wording: they sometimes hesitate, correct themselves, or ask others for help. It is clear that over the months and years of being read to, children learn many of the subtle details of behavior and speaking that go with reading a book. They become aware, for example, that the reader does not make up words—that a book has its own precise and unchanging set of words.

When children begin to attend to print, as well as pictures, in their attempts to read, several changes take place. They usually discover that they must read each individual word on a page. Realizing that they do not know how to decode more than a handful of familiar words, they may refuse to pretend to read anymore and may rely on others to read to them. Over a period of weeks and months, and often in connection with instruction on how to figure out letter and word sounds, children begin to try out strategies for decoding print. Unlike their earlier pretend reading, their reading now sounds choppy and disfluent, reflecting their enormous efforts to "break the code" of printed symbols.

These steps in pretend reading are not discrete stages that all children go through in a systematic progression, but reflect developmental patterns observed in many children as they move toward actual reading. Pretend reading allows children to role-play, to reenact and try out behaviors, skills, and thinking processes that are part of reading. This long period of play brings children very close to actual reading.

BEGINNING TO READ

Many children become interested in and curious about the written word at an early age. In the beginning, children have only a vague understanding of the correspondence between print on the page and the words they hear when someone reads. Gradually, they develop two complementary strategies that help them in the early stages of decoding print.

The first strategy is to pay attention to context cues—to rely on the location, the form of the print, and any accompanying graphic logos to help signal what the print says, such as STOP on a road sign or the name of a favorite cereal. As the experiences of children in Trackton demonstrate, young children can develop a "sight" vocabulary—that is, they can learn to read a number of words from context cues alone. The second strategy is based on phonics: children begin to learn letter-sound correspondences and use their working knowledge of letter sounds to figure out words. For months and even years, young children move back and forth between these two approaches to deciphering print, and often they rely more heavily on one than on the other. Many children's preference for one strategy over the other depends on whether they are more attuned to auditory or visual stimuli.

During the preschool years, children often make concrete and physical correspondences between print and the objects it stands for.[21] Children first assume that print represents a physical object such as a tree, chair, or person, but do not understand that it also can refer to an invisible state of mind such as "remembering." This assumption of physical correspondence can be seen in other ways. One boy said that "cat" could be written

OIA and "kittens" would be OAIOAIOAI. In his thinking, words for similar objects will naturally look similar (even though the words do not have similar sounds), and a word that refers to just one object must have fewer letters than a word referring to more than one. Young children may also have a concrete physical sense of relationship between letters and sounds. In the early stages, they employ the same letter-name strategy they use in invented spelling: they think that letters mark syllables rather than individual speech sounds in a word. Thus, a child might use one letter to write the word "chicken" and two letters to write the word "fencepost" because they hear two distinct words when pronouncing "fencepost."[22]

The phonetic strategy can simultaneously guide children's early writing and reading efforts. Ryan wrote the following story at age 5½, when he could not yet read conventionally:[23]

WSLEDLEBYAHSEGDALT
GDAEDLBYA.

He read this story to his teacher two days in a row and read it the same way both times. This suggests that he understood the permanency of print in representing a text: his writing created a text he could "read" more than once. When he read the story aloud, he placed his finger under the letter or letters that represented a word, and moved his finger along as he read. There was no punctuation in his written narrative, but he used appropriate pauses in his oral reading:

WS (Once) LE (there) (was a) DLE (little) BY (boy) A (and) H (one day) H (he) S (saw) E (a) GDALT (ghost) (that) GD (ghost) AE (ate) DL (little) BYA (boys).

In this story, Ryan uses one to three letters to represent each word, and for three relatively unimportant words, "was," "a," and "that," there is no representation at all. Words that are clearly of one syllable are represented by one letter: "A H H S E" ("and one day he saw a"). Ryan's teacher suggests that he may have used so many letters to write the word "ghost" because the word represents the central idea of his story and therefore deserves visual prominence.

Glenda Bissex reported that her son Paul developed both visual context and phonics strategies for reading, which he used in different situations and independently throughout the early stages of beginning to read. The first two words he could read were his name and EXIT, which he saw on highway signs during rides in the car. Until he was almost 6 years old, Paul read individual words everywhere around him; his main reading materials were labels, signs, book titles, and picture captions, rather than books.

In contrast, during this same period of time, Paul was writing sustained texts (stories, instructions, newspaper reports), using invented spellings that relied heavily on his knowledge of phonics. He learned about letter-sound relationships from watching *Sesame Street* in his preschool years, and from asking his parents how to spell certain words that he wanted to write. When he was writing, each letter with its sound was his unit of analysis; when he was reading print in his environment, whole words were his unit of analysis. When Paul turned 5, he made a discovery: "Once you know how to spell something, you know how to read it!" (p. 122). Thus Paul's reading between the ages of 5 and 6 was guided by phonics when he read the texts he wrote himself, and by context cues when he read words and short phrases he saw in the world around him.

When Paul was about 5½, he seemed to abandon the use of context cues and to rely more heavily on phonics strategies in his attempts to read. It was as if he felt a need to focus on these skills in order to master them. When he tried to read his first book, he felt frustrated because he needed help from his parents with words he could not sound out. Just before he turned 6, he read his first complete book on his own, P. D. Eastman's *Go, Dog, Go!* At this point he seemed to integrate his strategies, using what he knew about context (what made sense in terms of the meaning of the passage); using syntax (grammatical structures of sentences); using memory of the story from past readings; using picture cues; using cues from the initial and final letters of words along with knowledge of individual letter-sound relationships within words. From age 6 on, Paul could read simple books, enjoy them, and begin to explore the wealth and diversity of books available to a young reader. And he was well prepared for this exploration by the diversity of his strategies for finding meaning in a text.

In her review of the literature on beginning readers, Bissex found repeated confirmation that more successful readers were those who brought multiple strategies to their reading. Experts on reading also tell us that readers succeed better if provided with books that have exciting words and ideas, as opposed to those written with a tightly controlled vocabulary and uninteresting plots and characters. They are also likely to do better with books that call for the use of more than one reading strategy.[24]

Much instruction in reading focuses on children's skills in discriminating letters and identifying words, because these are the pieces of the reading process that are easiest to measure with standardized tests. Sometimes these skills are equated with reading itself, but this is a limited and misleading view. If reading is conceived of only as decoding, children may come to believe that reading consists of saying the individual words so they sound right, as opposed to understanding that reading is a "process of interpreting the world." Interpretation involves two people, the writer and the reader, with a desire to communicate, and the use of a system of agreed upon conventions (print) to convey and explore the meaning of ideas.[25]

Close observation of young children learning to read suggests that they thrive on richness and diversity of reading material, that they need time to develop and try out various strategies for decoding and interpreting print, and that they need months of practice on their own as well as continuing participation in reading activities with others, particularly being read to.

Our emphasis here on early experiences with print and reading is not meant to discount the important role of school in teaching children to read. Most children need the steady and consistent guidance from adults that usually comes with formal schooling to help them figure out the specifics of an alphabetic symbol system and how it works. Most children, however, begin school with some knowledge of print and the process of reading. Early experience with print in the environment, with being read to, with seeing adults read, and with playing with reading can prepare children for the reading instruction to come.

Long before school begins, children can benefit from knowing why people read and what people are doing when they read, and from receiving written messages and stories that make the experience of reading personally meaningful to them. It is remarkable how much children can learn, and how hard some children will work to break the code when they see the rewards of reading and are motivated to become readers themselves.

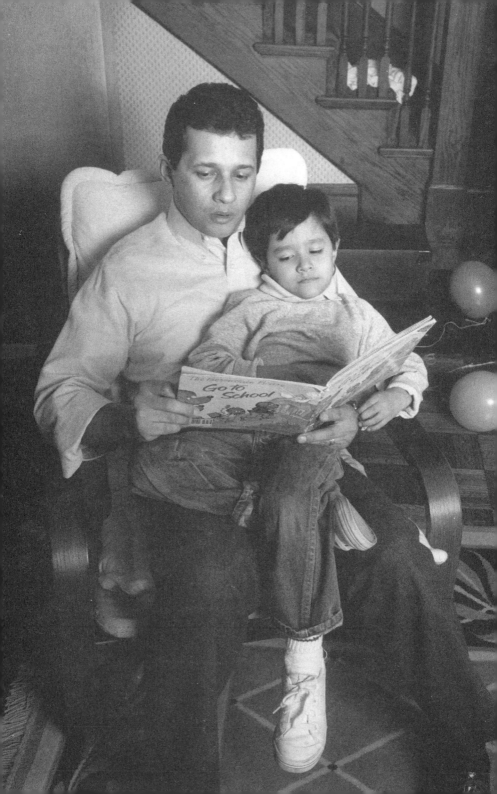

5/ At Home and in the Neighborhood

Children learn to write and read in the context of their closest social relationships. Parents—and sometimes other family members or friends—play several important roles in introducing young children to literacy. At the most basic level, parents and other family members give children access to *materials* for writing and reading. In a literate society like ours, print seems to be everywhere, and most children are exposed to a considerable amount in their homes and neighborhoods. Researchers have found a great deal of print in the homes of families from a variety of social and economic backgrounds, including low-income minority families. The packages of most foods, medicines, and cosmetics are covered with print; newspapers and magazines (usually including a TV guide) are present in most homes; even television displays large amounts of print, particularly during commercials. Moreover, many homes receive a steady stream of junk mail; as one observer remarked, "print does not merely reside in a household but rather flows through it."[1]

The availability of tools and materials for reading and writing certainly fosters early literacy development, and a lack of such materials, particularly books, is sometimes associated with a lack of literacy. But the equation is not a simple one. Asian refugee children observed by Bambi Schieffelin were able to make good use of school instruction without having many books or writing materials in their homes, and some inner-city black families observed by Joan McLane engaged in intensive reading and writing activities with a relatively restricted range of materials.[2] Although access to books and writing implements certainly contributes to early literacy development, there is no evidence that it is essential. What probably matters more is how printed materials and writing tools are used by adults, how they are made available to children, and what messages about their use and importance are communicated to young children.

Parents and other family members and friends influence the development of literacy by serving as *models* of literate behavior. Young children pay close attention to what they see the powerful and significant people in their world doing, and they imitate behaviors that seem to be important to these people. Children want to please their parents and older siblings, and they want to be like them and do what they do. But modeling is not the only way parents can communicate the importance, meaning, and value of literacy. Children in the Asian refugee families studied by Schieffelin did not often see their parents reading books or reading or writing in English, but these parents *did* communicate the importance of literacy in other ways. What may matter most is what parents communicate to their children in direct interactions involving writing and reading.

Parents (and others) *participate* in a range of writing and reading activities with young children. Parents may organize such activities, or children may initiate them themselves. These activities may be conducted casually and playfully, or they may be structured as deliberate, work-like situations. In these activities, parents convey bits of information, knowledge, and skills related to writing and reading. And, perhaps more important, they communicate significant messages about the value and importance of writing and reading, and about the child as a potential writer and reader.

Some parents encourage children's *play* and *fantasy*, including pretend writing and reading. As discussed in Chapter 2, playful uses of reading and writing indicate that children consider these to be important and interesting activities, worth imitating and investigating. Such play also provides clues to what children know about writing and reading, how they feel about writing and reading, and what they assume and expect about themselves as writers and readers.

Finally, some parents *read aloud*—and talk about—books with their children. Being read to is a central experience in many children's early literacy development (see Chapter 4). When children are read to frequently, books provide them with a rich source of stories and elaborate language, of ideas and fantasies, which they then use to create their own stories and enrich their pretend play.

In interactions with their parents (and others) involving writing and reading, children are not passive recipients of information; rather, they are active participants who want to learn to use and control writing and reading and make them their own. Children not only want to imitate and please adults; they also, at times, want to resist and assert themselves. This means that the dynamics of early literacy development are as complex as those in other areas of children's development: a child's response in any particular interaction depends on many factors, including the child's temperament, personality, and earlier experience, as well as the relationship in which the interaction takes place.[3]

The reading and writing activities of several children have been scrutinized in case studies—some conducted by parents—which chart the children's literacy development over several months or even years. Because case studies are necessarily restricted to a small number of children, they cannot claim to describe typical development. Nonetheless, there is much to be learned from these studies, which provide vivid, intimate details of parents and children involved in reading and writing. Case studies have been carried out in diverse settings, including college-educated, middle-class families, low-income inner-city black families, and Asian refugee families. These cultural groups organize writing and reading in different ways, so that young children participate in different kinds of early literacy activities and receive somewhat different messages about what it means to become literate, and about themselves as potential writers and readers.[4]

RACHEL, JOSHUA, JENNIFER, AND JILL

The reading and writing activities that take place in the homes and neighborhoods of college-educated middle-class professional families often seem ordinary and unremarkable because they are so informal and so much a part of the ongoing stream of family life. They are not labeled or thought of as "lessons"—or even as "literacy activities"—rather, they are simply things parents and children do with each other or by themselves. Children engage in activities related to literacy as part of their everyday lives and as part of their relationships with their parents, siblings, and friends.

The parents whose children have been the subject of case studies include teachers, social workers, college professors, a freelance writer, and a rock musician. These adults use writing and reading in their work as well as for information and personal pleasure. They clearly value literacy, and it has a central place in their lives, but because they take it for granted they may not pay much conscious attention to its importance. Thus, these parents may think that they are not teaching their children about writing and reading, and that their pre-school children do not need instruction in writing and reading—but they nevertheless are communicating attitudes, values, assumptions, and expectations as well as information about written language, giving their children a great deal of informal "instruction." As a consequence, children in such families gradually acquire not only knowledge and skills necessary for literacy, but, perhaps even more important, a sense of entitlement to literacy that enables them to see themselves as writers and readers long before they can actually write and read.

The homes of these families usually contain a great many books, as well as magazines and newspapers. The tools of literacy—books, paper, pencils—are likely to be as familiar and as accessible to children as dolls, blocks, toy cars and trucks, and "transformers." Children are given books as presents, often from birth, and they gradually accumulate libraries of their own, which may be supplemented by regular trips to the local public library. These children have a variety of writing tools of their own, such as pencils, crayons, markers, paper, rubber stamps with letters on them, and wooden and magnetic letters; some may even have access to typewriters and computers. They feel free to use these materials as part of their everyday play—they look at books or magazines, and use pencils or crayons to scribble, draw, or write. They explore, experiment, and play with literacy materials on their own and with family members and friends.

These children also see their parents reading books, newspapers, and magazines for pleasure and for information, and hear them talking about what they read; they see their parents writing down phone messages, writing letters, paying bills, and sometimes working on articles or books, and hear them talking about their writing. From an early age, they know that reading and writing are important adult activities.

Rachel, age 3, had seen both her parents do a great deal of writing, including writing books and articles. One day she sat down at a small table in the kitchen. On the table were a telephone, pads of paper, a pen, and some pencils. Rachel took the pen and scribbled wavy lines on several pieces of paper and then announced in a loud voice: "Be quiet! I'm working at my desk!" On another occasion, Rachel went into her bedroom and put some paper and some markers on a small table and said "Don't bother me. I'm working in my study." Then she closed the door.

When children imitate their parents and other significant people in their lives, they are likely to gain elementary understandings of the activity they are imitating. Rachel's playful scribbling suggests that she has some general notions of what writing is—she knows, for example, that it involves making patterned marks on paper. Moreover, Rachel has come to regard the activity of writing as interesting and the role of writer as one worth emulating; indeed, she regards it as an important and powerful one that carries certain adult privileges (such as telling other people to be quiet). Observation and imitation are ways for children to make sense of what they see going on around them; they are also an important part of the process by which young children incorporate the attitudes, values, expectations, and assumptions of the people who are important in their lives.

Children in these families also participate in reading and writing activities with their parents. These often appear casual and playful, and they are as likely to be initiated by the children as by the adults. Parents (and older siblings or other family members) sometimes serve as assistants and instructors, providing children with materials and technical help with reading and writing, and sometimes serve as audiences for children's literary performances and productions.

The mother of 4-year-old Joshua reported that one evening he used his typewriter to type what looked like a random assortment of letters, numbers, and symbols on both sides of a piece of paper. He said these bits of writing were "Goldilocks and the Three Bears," "Snow White and the Three Dwarfs," "The Three Billy Goats Gruff," and "The Brementown Musicians." While typing these "stories," Joshua took the paper out of the typewriter every few minutes and ran up and down the stairs to show each parent what he had added to the page. He was clearly very proud of himself, and at one point shouted with glee, "I can read! I can write!" Several times he announced, "I did it all myself! Nobody helped me!"

Joshua continued this activity early the next morning, typing on both sides of another sheet of paper. This time he said he had written "Mary Had a Little Lamb." His father "read" one side of the page as "Mary had a little lamb." Joshua corrected him by taking the paper and reading it himself as "Mary had a little—turn the page over [which he did]—lamb." Joshua's use of titles of fairy tales (and a nursery rhyme) to label and define his bits of writing shows that he had learned something about the conventional forms of written language. Perhaps what is most striking in this activity is Joshua's delight in playing the role of writer and reader, his pleasure in acting *as if* he could write and read—and his father's participation in his pretend writing and reading. Joshua's parents did not tell him that his writing was unreadable gibberish. Instead, they accepted his interpretations of what he wrote as he presented them. It seems likely that such a response fostered Joshua's emerging sense of himself as a writer and reader, and encouraged him to continue his experiments with writing and reading.

In treating such a rough approximation of writing and reading as if it were the real thing, Joshua's father was responding in much the same spirit in which most parents respond to their baby's babblings and early vocalizations. As Jerome Bruner and others have pointed out, most parents do not correct their infant's very rough approximations of mature speech; rather, they respond with pleasure and often supply sympathetic interpretations of what they think their child is trying to say; and this encourages their children to keep on trying—and learning—to talk.[5] This means that infants learning to talk try out and experiment with the sounds they are learning, in the context of supportive interactions with adults. Similarly, when parents respond to their children's approximations of writing and reading with enthusiasm and appreciation, they are giving their children support that is likely to encourage further exploration and experimentation with literacy.

Parents in these case-study families enjoyed and encouraged their children's fantasy and pretend play, as well as their play with language, writing, and reading.

Their children engaged in a great deal of play—pretend play, role-playing, fantasy, language play, and games—and brought writing and reading into their play in many ways. Sometimes they used books or writing materials as part of the action in dramatic play or as props in a dramatic performance; sometimes their play scenarios were based on a favorite storybook; sometimes writing and reading served as extensions of pretend play and fantasy, as they did when 4-year-old Joshua made a sign to hang on his bedroom door.

Joshua asked his mother to give him a piece of paper and a pencil and to tell him "the letters that spell *danger*." His mother asked why and Joshua replied that he wanted "to make a danger sign" to put on the door of his room. Then he told his mother "an involved and changing story" about various catastrophes that had happened in his room, which explained why "there was a hole in his floor." After describing each catastrophe—"a bear tore my room up; a tree fell down; there's a monster up there"—he would say "Really, Mommy. Really, that's true." His mother gave him a pencil and paper, and told him to start with D. She reported that he had "much trouble writing it, but I assured him it was a D. A was easy, N was shaky, and he absolutely refused to try G and insisted that I write it for him. E was a breeze, and he asked me to do the R." They found some string and some tape and made a handle so the sign could hang on Joshua's door, where it stayed for the rest of the day. Periodically, Joshua would ask his mother if anyone had been in his room. "Nobody can go in here but me," he would say, "because there's danger in there."

Here, as on other occasions, Joshua's mother demonstrated her willingness to go along with her son's fantastic tales, rather than dismissing them as lies or nonsense. In doing this, she was encouraging him to construct an imaginary "possible world" of his own devising—and helping him to use writing to extend and elaborate on his construction.

These parents also read to their children often, and talk about the characters and plots in the books they read. When this happens, books seem to permeate children's relationships—and their playful interactions—with the significant people in their lives.

Jennifer's parents had begun reading to her when she was about 6 months old. One weekend when Jennifer was 2 she went with her father to visit her grandmother in the country. Her grandmother read her *Johnny Lion's Book* by Edith Thacher Hurd—a storybook about a young lion who dreams about going hunting in the woods. About an hour later, Jennifer, who had been playing outside, called to her father, "I read a book, Daddy." She held two big leaves she had picked, one lying flat on the palm of each hand. She and her father sat down on the front steps, side by side, and Jennifer started "reading" her "book" in what her grandmother described as a "dramatic voice," which *sounded* very much like reading. "And a big bear (pause) went into the woods and she saw a big lion (pause) and she chased a big lion (pause) and she caught a big lion." After another pause, her father said, "and then what did the big bear do?" Jennifer answered, "Then the big bear went home to her mommy."

By the age of 2—long before she knew how to decode written language—Jennifer was so familiar with the activity of reading a book that two leaves could serve as her "text" and she could invent a simple but coherent story and tell it in a voice that accurately mimicked a reading intonation. This exchange also suggests that Jennifer found reading interesting and pleasurable—as well as a good way to capture her father's attention. She expected her father to appreciate her literary performance, and he did, entering into her pretense as a receptive audience. He also helped her find an ending to her story, perhaps intuitively letting her know that stories *should* have endings. In doing this, he was accepting his daughter's playful, nonliteral performance as it was presented, and then using it to expand her knowledge about literacy.

Many children also find support for literacy among siblings and friends. Older children help younger siblings and friends with writing and reading, providing assistance and instruction, encouraging playful uses of writing and reading, and sometimes serving as co-conspirators or as competitors.

One day Jill, age 5, and her 7-year-old sister, Nina, playing together, concocted a "magic potion."[6] Nina suggested they write down the ingredients; she found paper and pencil and wrote a list, then helped Jill spell the words so she could make her own list (the invented spellings are Nina's):

POCION
UNGRINE PEPER, HAIR + HONEY + e GARLICK

Nina used her more sophisticated knowledge of spelling to help Jill carry out a writing task she would not have been able to complete on her own, and she did this by adapting her assistance to her younger sister's level of competence.

Nina and Jill also used writing in surreptitious activities. On one occasion, they made a series of scatalogical "mixed media"—combinations of drawing and writing—about a boy in the neighborhood they didn't like. Nina directed this activity so that Jill did all the drawing and writing, with Nina once again supplying the spellings.

During a summer vacation, the sisters discovered an-other secretive and conspiratorial use for writing when 9-year-old Jeannie recruited them and several other friends in her suburban neighborhood—all but Jill were 7-year-olds—to form a "spying club." Jeannie set the rules and ran the meetings. Club members were to sneak around the neighborhood, watch what people were doing, write this down, and then bring their "spies" to the next meeting. Each member was supplied with paper and pencil. Then a problem came up: Jill wanted to play but did not know how to write. The club agreed that Jill would either go with one of the older children and help her spy, or spy on her own and then find another club member to write down her "spy." This game caught on and was played with enthusiasm for the rest of the summer. During the next winter Jill and Nina continued to write occasional "spies" (such as DAD IS TALKING TO MOM), Nina again helping Jill with spellings. Sometime the following spring, Jill asked her mother to help her write a "spy" (on her mother):

MOM   IS
FOLDING
CLOTH
ES

These children were using writing and reading as part of a peer-directed group activity. A "spying club" seems well designed to meet school-age children's need for group membership and identity, and their need to in-vent their own rules of behavior. It also gives them the satisfaction of keeping secrets from adults. Spying is a secretive, forbidden activity which implies power over those who are spied upon. The use of writing to record their spying suggests that these children recognized value and power in written language, and that they had found a compelling way to make it their own.

Nina and Jill appeared to enjoy cooperating and playing the roles of expert/teacher and beginner/learner. They did not always cooperate, however. For example, one time when Nina was writing a "book about plants," Jill wanted to make one too. She tried to do this by herself, and was not pleased with the result because Nina's writing skills were so much more advanced than her own. Jill ended up feeling frustrated and incompetent, acutely aware of her inferiority as a writer. In this case writing had become an arena for competition between siblings.

Joshua also engaged in conspiratorial writing activities with friends. For example, when he and his friend Mark were 7 years old, they made lists of "suspicious" people in the neighborhood in a small notebook. Typical entries:

1 people
5 people

On another occasion, Joshua and Mark spent much of an afternoon, each laboriously copying a page from a book (Joshua from a child's version of *Great Tales from the Bible* and Mark from a book of children's stories entitled *Me and Clara*). Joshua's mother reported there was "much giggling" while they were doing this. When they finished, they delivered their pages of text as "letters" to a boy who lived across the street, putting them under a rock on the front doorstep of his house. Joshua and Mark thought they were playing an enormous joke on this boy, whom they didn't much like. (The boy's reaction is not known.) In this instance, written language was a crucial part of a (somewhat obscure) practical joke.

Copying a page of text would be an onerous task for most 7-year-olds if assigned as schoolwork, but as a self-initiated task under their own direction and control, it was a hilarious activity for these two boys.

In using writing and reading for secretive activities like spying and playing jokes, these children were finding a place for literacy in relationships with their siblings and friends. At the same time, they were exercising and perhaps expanding their literacy skills, and strengthening their sense of ownership of writing and reading. These activities also attest to the pervasiveness of literacy in their lives.

BENJAMIN AND TIFFANIE

Early literacy activities are not always so casual and playful. Some parents give their children more consciously organized and lesson-like introductions to reading and writing. McLane found this to be the case in five low-income black families who live in small apartments in a poor, inner-city neighborhood in Chicago. The adults in these families are either on welfare or have low-paying jobs. None has completed college, and some did not finish high school. All of them devote considerable time and effort to working with their children on reading and writing skills.

One of these parents, Phyllis Jones, reads a great deal and owns many books. She frequently buys magazines and newspapers, and believes it is important for her son to see her reading. Her son, Benjamin, has been given books since he was an infant; he also has access to crayons, pencils, and paper. In the other four families there are far fewer books for either adults or children, and few writing materials, particularly for children's use.

Children in these families observe varying amounts of

writing and reading in their homes. Benjamin often sees his mother reading; another child, Tiffanie, sees her mother writing and reading as part of her course work for a community college; Tiffanie and other children see their older siblings working on homework assignments. All of these children also see their parents writing and reading for a variety of practical tasks, such as filling out financial forms and reading the newspaper.

Phyllis Jones is unemployed and lives on welfare with Benjamin. She finished high school and two years of college, and regrets that she did not go farther. She wishes she had "listened to her grandmother" who was "always pushing" her to study; instead, "I did enough just to get by." She is deeply concerned about her son's education, and determined that he will go farther than she did. She is particularly concerned about his learning to read, noting that "without reading, you can't do anything," and that "readers are leaders—I want Benjamin to read and read and read." She has little trust in the local public schools, and is acutely aware of the large numbers of poor black children who fail to learn to read well and who drop out of school: "I guess black people have a tendency to just say 'Oh, I can't do it, I can't do it, I can't do it.' "

Mrs. Jones decided that the only way to be certain that Benjamin would learn to read was to teach him herself. She began buying books for him when he was an infant, and she asked friends and relatives to give him books as Christmas and birthday presents. Before he turned 3, she bought him a set of phonics tapes and workbooks, which she used to conduct regular lessons, helping Benjamin learn to recognize the forms and sounds of letters, combinations of letters, and eventually entire words. She also gave him lessons in letter formation, handwriting, and spelling. When Benjamin was 3, he began attending a Head Start program, while his mother continued to teach him at home. She tried to make these activities "fun for Benjamin." She was pleased with his interest in reading and writing, and sometimes frustrated that he did not learn as quickly as she wanted him to.

Benjamin sometimes pretended to read magazines, newspapers, and books. His mother was gratified by his enthusiasm, commenting on his "reading" of *The Gingerbread Man,* "you can hear the laughter and joy in his voice." But she also told Benjamin he was "not really reading." On one occasion, she pointed to the print in the book Benjamin was pretending to read and said "these are what you read. Someday you will learn to read." Another time she commented, "Benjamin thinks he can read. What he'll do is recite some words from a story and exclaim with great joy 'I can read! I can read!' I explained to him that he isn't reading. Reading is looking at a book and saying the words that are written there. But I say one day he will read—soon, just like Tony [an older friend of Benjamin's]." By the time Benjamin was 4, his mother noted that he knew "all of his alphabet by sight. Praise God!"

When Benjamin turned 4, Mrs. Jones began taking him to a reading program at the storefront church she attended. This program was designed for older children, but she thought he would "pick up something." She also continued to work on reading and writing at home, using index cards to make a card game to teach Benjamin how to write his name. When he was about 4½, Benjamin began sounding out words that he noticed around him, such as "off" and "on." His mother commented, "now he wants to know what everything spells and wants to guess at some of them. He asked me on the bus if E-M-E-R-G-E-N-C-Y spelled 'emergency'."

On another occasion, when she picked Benjamin up at Head Start, "he said 'Guess what we did today? I'll give you a hint—it begins with J. Then he said the word was J-E-M, which was supposed to be 'gym'." His mother was delighted with his interest in reading: "Hurrah! I hope it carries through the rest of his life." By the end of his second year in Head Start, when he had just turned 5, Benjamin could read a number of simple words by sounding them out and had a small sight vocabulary. His mother took great pride in these achievements: "Hallelujah! He can read!"

Ernestine Taylor, who is also poor and black and on welfare, lives in a sparsely furnished apartment in a rough inner-city neighborhood. She has six children. The two oldest boys, in their late teens, have both been in trouble with the law, and her oldest daughter, who is 16, is in trouble "on the streets"; her 8-year-old sons are "just getting by" in school; her youngest child, 5-year-old Tiffanie, is doing well in kindergarten. Mrs. Taylor shares many of Mrs. Jones's regrets about her own education, as well as similar anxieties and hopes for her children's education. She did not finish high school, and now wishes she had "listened" to her parents when she was younger and regrets her failure to "plan ahead." She said of her own schooling, "I really didn't take the time . . . I fooled around too much. Sometimes I really hate that . . . that I really didn't sit there in school like I should have." Soon after Tiffanie began attending a Head Start program, Mrs. Taylor began taking a course at a community college, training to become a medical assistant. She found this difficult and challenging, commenting that "it opened up my mind." She has plans to get her GED certificate, and eventually to become a registered nurse.

Like Mrs. Jones, Mrs. Taylor worries about the lure of

life "out on the streets" and the possibility that her younger children will "mess up," as she thinks her older children have. She worries about negative peer influences and the dangers of gangs, drugs, and teenage pregnancy. She has little faith in the local public schools, and thinks that many of the teachers are "prejudiced against people of color." She is discouraged about her older children's school experiences and their low achievement, and she is determined that her youngest child will do better.

Mrs. Taylor was eager for Tiffanie to learn to read and write, and, like Benjamin's mother, she believed that the only way to be certain that Tiffanie would learn was to teach her herself. Beginning when Tiffanie was about 3½, her mother began buying reading readiness workbooks and teaching her letters and sounds. By the time she was 4½, Tiffanie could write "ABC's from memory"; by the time she was 5, she could write her name and read simple children's stories. When Tiffanie engaged in writing or reading activities at home, her mother watched and listened carefully, supplying words that Tiffanie couldn't sound out for herself, telling her to take her time, or to start over, telling her to erase letters when she made a mistake, and sometimes urging her to hurry up and complete a task. Mrs. Taylor was proud of her daughter's reading ability, and was eager to show off her literacy skills to interested adults (such as the Head Start teacher and the researcher): "She can write. She can read too." By the time Tiffanie was five, she and her mother were reading the Bible together every day, with Tiffanie reading the "easy" words and her mother the "hard" ones: "The hard words I tell her but the rest she gets." Mrs. Taylor did this both to improve Tiffanie's reading skills and to instruct her in "the word of God." At the end of the school year, Tiffanie's kindergarten teacher reported that she was doing well in school literacy tasks.

We do not know how common such an emphasis on literacy is among poor black families, and Phyllis Jones and Ernestine Taylor (and the other parents in McLane's study) may not be typical "welfare mothers." But their involvement and commitment challenge the stereotypical notion that low-income minority parents are unconcerned about their children's literacy development.

These inner-city families show a different pattern of early literacy development from that in the middle-class professional families described earlier. Because these parents feel that they cannot take literacy for granted, they deliberately organize reading and writing activities for their children, which often resemble school lessons.[7] These parents do not seem particularly interested in or comfortable with their children's playful approaches to writing and reading, and many of Benjamin and Tiffanie's early experiences with literacy appear to be more like work than like play. But the parents do communicate pleasure and pride in their children's achievements with writing and reading. We do not know whether literacy is part of these children's play with their friends. The neighborhoods they live in are considered dangerous, and they are not allowed much freedom to go outside to play with other children. Because of this, their reading and writing activities are likely to be confined to the family setting.

CHILDREN IN ASIAN REFUGEE FAMILIES

Bambi Schieffelin observed children's experiences with literacy in a community of Sino-Vietnamese refugees in Philadelphia. These families, who were recent arrivals from Vietnam, lived under generally stressful conditions, working long hours and living in crowded apartments. Parents did not buy books for their children and did not read to them, there were few books or other reading materials in the home, and most of these were in Cantonese. As far as we know, these parents did not encourage or engage in playful literacy activities with their children. Moreover, these parents did not speak, read, or write much English, so they could not help their children with school literacy tasks. Nevertheless, their children were able to make good use of school instruction and made "remarkable progress" in learning to read and write.[8]

One part of the explanation for this success is that these children sought help with writing and reading from English-speaking adults outside their families. To do this, they established a network of relationships outside the home, using support services available at school, at church, and elsewhere in the community. They received help from teachers, social workers, neighborhood organizations, and their family sponsors (many refugee families had American families as sponsors). Some children used a "homework hotline" (a service established for refugee children), which allowed them to telephone tutors about their schoolwork.

Another part of the explanation is that the Sino-Vietnamese culture places a high value on literacy and schooling: these parents presumably communicated this value to their children in a variety of ways.[9] One way they did this was by writing and reading letters to and from relatives in Vietnam; reading letters aloud was a frequent and important family event. Another way some of these parents indicated the value they placed on education, according to Schieffelin, was to tell school authorities that their children were two or three years

younger than they actually were. They used this strategy to ensure that their children received as many years
of education as possible.

Perhaps as important, these children were frequently
asked to help their parents and other family members
with writing and reading. They assisted their parents
and other relatives with literacy tasks such as translating and reading notes from school, writing notes to
school, and filling out medical, financial, and job-related
forms. Such "literacy role reversals" may have made
these Asian children particularly conscious of the importance of being literate and of the value of their own
developing competence in reading and writing.

Playing a significant role in bringing English-language
literacy to their parents seemed to give some of these
children a unique sense of the power that writing and
reading can confer. Schieffelin noted that Asian school
children often mentioned literacy skills in letters to pen
pals and in the stories they wrote in school; their native-
English-speaking classmates did not do this. For example, V., a Sino-Vietnamese boy from Saigon, who began
his American schooling in second grade, wrote the following story at the age of 9:

> the magic book January 5, 1981
> Once upon time. there was a boy. the
> boy was named Peter. Peter went out
> to play. with his friend. his friend
> named Joe. then Joe and Peter walk
> then Peter and Joe find a magic book
> then Peter and Joe look inside of
> the book. then they don't know how to
> read. the magic words. then they go
> to aske the man. the man said this
> book is a magic book. then they

> wish they can read. then the
> book said your wish is my
> command. then they can read.[10]

For many 9-year-old boys, magical power is likely to be associated with great physical strength, such as the prowess of superheroes or high-tech weapons. For V., however, magical power is associated with literacy. In "the magic book," V. may be expressing his sense of control and ownership of writing and reading, much as other children may express such feelings when they play with writing and reading.

LITERACY AND RELATIONSHIPS

As we have seen, for some children literacy begins early—well before formal school instruction in writing and reading. Such early literacy development is closely tied to children's relationships with the significant people in their lives. Parents, and sometimes siblings and friends, offer young children a range of resources and supports for early literacy development. These supports reflect attitudes, assumptions, and expectations about literacy, as well as particular circumstances (such as living in a neighborhood with poor schools, or being recent immigrants in a strange country). It is in relationships with people who matter that values, meanings, and expectations, as well as knowledge, information, and skills, are enacted and communicated.

The parents of the children we have discussed have strong relationships with their children. They spend time with them, worry about them, scold them, teach them, play with them, and enjoy them. To these relationships, parents bring their own interests in reading and writing and their sense of themselves as readers and writers, as well as their hopes and expectations (which may be conscious or unconscious) about their children as potential readers and writers. All of these factors affect how parents organize literacy activities for their children, how they transmit information about writing and reading, and what attitudes about literacy they communicate to their children.

When questioned about their role in their children's literacy development, these parents responded in different ways. When the case study of Joshua began (he had just turned 4), both his mother and his father expressed skepticism at the notion that they were doing anything to encourage or help him learn to read and write. They said they were not aware they were promoting literacy learning, or in any way instructing their child about reading or writing—or that they needed to be doing so. Indeed, as in other middle-class professional families where literacy is both valued and taken for granted, these parents seemed to assume their child would become literate. Although Joshua did not learn to read until he was 7, his mother commented some years later (when he was 10) that she had "never had any doubt that he would learn to read." This confidence allowed these parents to take a casual and playful approach to their children's explorations of reading and writing. On closer observation, however, it became evident that in fact these parents were doing a great deal to foster their children's literacy development.

The mothers of Benjamin and Tiffanie, in contrast, were less confident about their children's learning to read and write. Benjamin's mother commented, "If you're not involved, then that would leave your kids free . . . to . . . begin to sink." To make sure that Benjamin did not "sink," his mother invested a great deal of energy in providing him with carefully planned literacy lessons. Her instruction, like that of Tiffanie's mother, took the form of deliberately planned tasks that resembled and anticipated school lessons. These parents gave their children explicit, didactic messages about the importance of becoming literate.

The refugee parents described by Schieffelin conveyed the importance and value they give to literacy by communicating their high expectations of their children's school experience, and by requesting assistance with writing and reading from their children. It seems likely that being able to help their parents with literacy tasks made these children particularly aware of the power and prestige that can come with being literate.

These case studies make it clear that early literacy can develop in more than one way, and that there is no single "literacy curriculum." Parents play a crucial role in children's early literacy development by providing materials, communicating assumptions and expectations, and giving help and instruction—all in the context of the most significant relationships children have. In different ways, from intuitive and playful collaboration to carefully organized instruction, parents (and sometimes other family members and friends) not only give children tools and opportunities for writing and reading, they also give them reasons to write and read, and reasons to want to master the skills needed for mature writing and reading.

6/ In Preschool and Kindergarten

When children leave home to go to preschool or kindergarten—or daycare, Head Start, or nursery school—they encounter new ways to learn about writing and reading. These early childhood programs can offer a range of planned activities, guided by teachers, that support literacy development. The processes of teaching and learning that take place in these settings look quite different from those in children's homes and neighborhoods, and also different from those in elementary school, where teachers provide lessons and children work quietly at desks.

Two assumptions shape our discussion of preschool and kindergarten. First, children learn about literacy most easily when writing and reading are embedded in daily classroom activities that have a purpose children can understand. And second, children are most likely to develop foundations for learning to read and write if they participate in what Robert Gundlach calls "a community of writers and readers":

> By participating in such a community, you stand a reasonably good chance of acquiring notions of style and genre, of developing a general sense of the literary enterprise, and of increasing your sophistication about the act of writing itself . . . we ought to be asking how teach-

ers can assemble true communities of active readers and writers, and how teachers can organize things so that even the most reluctant student has a clear shot at becoming a participating member.[1]

The learning of literacy is indeed a social process: children have a good chance of becoming writers and readers, and of becoming more sophisticated ones in time, if they use written language to communicate and interact with those they play and work with every day.

But how can teachers create a community of writers and readers with young children who cannot yet write and read? Traditional education has assumed that children need instruction in "basic skills" before they can begin to use writing and reading for communication and interaction. Judith Lindfors addresses this dilemma when she discusses James Britton's distinction between two meanings of the word "practice." The first meaning is rehearsal for a performance that will come later; such "practice isn't the real thing, it is rehearsal for the real thing." The second meaning is to engage in an activity, as for example when a doctor practices medicine or a lawyer practices law. This kind of practice *is* the real thing.[2]

Lindfors points out the inappropriateness of the first definition of "practice" when applied to children's oral language development. From the first year of life, "the child uses language in whatever ways she is able to in order to communicate her meanings and to interpret the expression of others; and in the process of engaging in language, her expression and understanding develop, becoming more elaborated, more conventional, more refined."[3] Right from the start, then, language for the young child is "doing communication," not preparing for communication. In recent years, this view of oral language development has begun to influence many educators' understanding of written language development. Not only spoken language but also early literacy can develop as a form of "engaging in practice" while children find ways to communicate using whatever level of literacy skill they have attained.

BASIC ACTIVITIES FOR LITERACY

The concept of "basic activities," developed by Michael Cole and Peg Griffin, provides a framework that can help us understand what children learn from participating in projects involving books, paper, and pencils in preschool and kindergarten classrooms.[4] Basic activities represent an alternative approach to "basic skills," or the "rehearsal" type of practice that has traditionally dominated early instruction in reading and writing. Basic literacy activities involve children in reading and writing for a purpose the children can comprehend; they involve children at various levels of skill and understanding; and they allow children to take control of the task when they are ready to do so. Basic activities capitalize on the active and social nature of children's learning and on children's interest in play, particularly pretend play with their peers. They also allow adults to involve children in using writing and reading skills for a variety of purposes, and to demonstrate how these skills work in the course of activities that make sense to children. Thus a focus on basic activities does not discount the importance of basic skills; on the contrary, children are exposed to, learn, and eventually master skills in a meaningful context.

There is no one way to "package" basic activities in an early literacy program. There are, however, several common ingredients that are likely to be found in preschool and kindergarten classrooms that support early literacy development. First, children have opportunities for fantasy play: play with other children, play with various kinds of materials (sand, water, clay, paints, paper, writing tools), and extended open-ended conversations with teachers and peers. Second, books and writing materials are accessible to children. There is usually a library area of the classroom with picture books displayed on shelves where children can see and reach them. There is often a comfortable place to sit and read nearby, and children are given time during the day to look at books and read them. Third, there is a table for drawing and writing in a central place, equipped with paper, crayons, markers, scissors, paste, and other inviting tools such as a stapler, a hole puncher, and rulers. Fourth, children are read to—they listen to a range of good stories, fairy tales, and poetry daily.

Classroom activities that develop from these ingredients can help prepare children for literacy in several ways. Daily opportunities for fantasy play are important because, as they play, children fashion possible worlds, create problems, invent solutions, and most important, do this through the use of symbols—particularly talk. Dramatic fantasy play among groups of children offers practice in expressing ideas verbally with precision and clarity. For example, a child says to a group of friends, "Pretend the princess and her friends go on a picnic in the forest and get lost. The wicked witch captures them and brings them to her hideout." Such statements create a story, an imaginary situation, and a set of premises for a problem. Another child says, "Pretend these checkers are our food and this rug is the forest and the table is the witch's house," thereby establishing agreed-upon symbols for acting out the story. The children then develop the imaginary situation: "OK, now it's time to go for our picnic. Who wants to eat potato chips? Here, baby, here's some for you. Uh-oh, here comes the witch. Let's hide behind this rock! Fee-fi-fo-fum, here I come! I smell something funny. Ah-ha! I caught you!"

Reading and writing involve a similar sort of fluency in using words to call up experiences not present in the immediate here and now. While reading and writing, one becomes absorbed in a world and events that are divorced from the present time and circumstances. Children's ability to create an imaginary text through play can eventually help them to create and comprehend written texts.

Books, paper, and writing tools have a central place in classrooms that support literacy development. During the preschool and kindergarten years, these materials are presented alongside many others in the classroom. By first grade, however, most other equipment disappears, and books, paper, and pencils remain the core of school activity. A table for drawing or writing, furnished with inviting tools for preschool and kindergarten children to use in open-ended ways, represents the essence of schooling. This table is the precursor to the school desks that children will sit at for many years to come as they write and read, and it holds many of the tools they will use at their desks. Through their scribbling, drawing, pretend writing, and invented spelling, children develop skills in the use of these tools as they gradually learn to represent their ideas on paper.

Other kinds of classroom experiences with written language, such as listening to stories and discussing them as a group, also help to prepare children for the writing and reading they will encounter in elementary school and beyond. Experiences with literacy in elementary school include creating, commenting on, and interpreting various kinds of texts: stories, accounts of events and ideas (for example, in social studies and history), and descriptions of procedures (for example, in science and mathematics). Reading books, stories, and poems daily and having open-ended discussions of the ideas they raise points children toward the book-oriented literacy around which schooling revolves.

The dictation of stories is another basic literacy activity that involves children in the writing process in a very direct way. The "language experience" or "whole language" approach to early reading instruction has long recognized the importance of giving children chances to have their stories and ideas put into writing by an adult scribe. Vivian Paley has taken this activity one step further by having children dictate stories and then having the class act them out.

According to Paley, the dictation of stories had always been available to children in her classroom, but only a handful of children (mostly girls) chose it over the course of the year. There was a boy named Wally in one of her kindergarten classes who often seemed to be in some kind of trouble. One day, after several upsets, trying to help Wally participate in classroom activities with a more positive outlook, Paley asked him if he would like to act out a story he had just dictated. Dramatizing the story had a remarkable effect on Wally—and on the entire class:

> It made Wally very happy, and a flurry of story writing began that continued and grew all year. The boys dictated as many stories as the girls, and we acted out each story the day it was written if we could.
>
> Before, we had never acted out these stories. We had dramatized every other kind of printed word—fairy tales, story books, poems, songs—but it had always seemed enough just to write the children's words. Obviously it was not; the words did not sufficiently repre-

sent the action, which needed to be shared. For this alone, the children would give up play time, as it was a true extension of play.[5]

Paley's work provides abundant evidence of how much children enjoy dictation once they realize that their stories will be acted out. We believe Paley has discovered an important literacy activity. Over the past several years, we have been studying story dictation and dramatization with children from various socioeconomic backgrounds in order to understand how these activities might contribute to early literacy development, particularly in children considered at risk for failure in school literacy tasks.

What follows is a look at basic literacy activities in progress in a classroom of kindergarten children in an after-school program. The teachers and administrators of this program have been working with us for several years, exploring the value of basic literacy activities for the children they teach. The teachers and children are black, and the classroom is part of a government-funded program in an inner-city community. The children attend half-day kindergarten in the local public school, and then attend this after-school daycare program at a neighborhood community center. In order to enroll their children, parents have to be going to school, involved in job training, or working. Most of the twenty children in this classroom previously attended Head Start for two years in the same community center. The Head Start classrooms also employ the concepts of basic literacy activities in their curriculum, so the children described here have been part of a literacy-rich preschool environment for several years now. The following observation occurred during a free-play activity time and the teacher-led group time that followed.

MISS ADAMS'S CLASSROOM

One afternoon in January, three boys are playing with an assortment of small toys on a table. They have some Lincoln logs, a few marbles, and a little plastic box. They tell their teacher that they are playing "the mouse" game. They make a sloping road and let the marble roll down it from different heights and angles. Their maze of roads soon includes a three-foot drop to the floor, and they carefully gauge where to put the plastic box so the "mouse" will fall into the "trap." The boys play with great concentration, experimenting with the materials, varying the arrangement each time, observing and adjusting the road to create new effects.

In time, a new game evolves, called "somebody shot him." Anthony and Timothy put the marble on the top of a magic marker lid and balance this on a Lincoln log plank suspended over the top of a carton. They gently flip the end of the Lincoln log to get the marble to fly off the magic marker top into the box. Later they put the little plastic box inside the carton and try to get the marble to land inside this too. Timothy says he wants to keep score. He runs to get a piece of paper and a pencil from a table nearby. Timothy writes across the top of his paper: 5 4 3 2 1 4 4 4 4. He puts a circle around each number except the last two. His numbers are correctly formed except the 5, which is backwards and upside down.

Anthony now wants his own piece of paper for writing scores, and he too gets paper from the drawing/writing table in the center of the classroom. Their teacher, Miss Adams, stops by their table to observe and ask them about their activities. She asks if they would like to dictate a story this afternoon. The boys respond with enthusiasm. Charlyne, a new girl who joined the class after Christmas, sits at the table watching the boys. Giving each child paper and pencil, the teacher suggests they draw pictures until it is their turn to dictate a story. Anthony is first and dictates the following story:

> Once upon a time it was two little boys. They mother left them. Then a stranger came in their house. He said, "Where your mama at?" "She at the store." Then he kidnapped them. Then he tied them up on ropes in the chair. Then they scoot their chair up to the telephone. Then there was a knife sitting on the side on the cabinet. They scoot their chair up to it. Then they cut themself unloose. Then they run back home. When mama got home, she told them to go to bed. The end.

Then Timothy has his turn:

> Once upon a time it was a Christmas tree. The boy had stole some bread and the mama said, "Where'd you get that bread from?" He said, "I stole it." He went outside when his mama told him to go to bed. He went over his friend house and took some of his friend's toys. His cousin come over to play with him and they went outside and play with his toys. His friend stole some more of his toys. And his friend went to the store and stole some toys. Somebody call the police and the boys went to jail. The end.

Both boys speak clearly and slowly, giving their teacher time to write down each sentence.

Miss Adams then asks Charlyne if she wants to tell a story. Miss Adams has asked her the same question a number of times during the past couple of weeks, but Charlyne has always said no. This time she answers excitedly, "Yes." While listening to the two boys, she has drawn a Christmas tree with a brightly colored box on it. Now she stands beside the teacher, ready to dictate her story.

Teacher: What's your story?

Charlyne: Tree door.

Teacher: Is that a tree with a door in it?

Charlyne: Yes.

Teacher: How nice! Is there more to your story?

Charlyne: (She takes her piece of paper and gets a crayon and draws a semicircle under the tree and a box under the semicircle. Then she hands the piece of paper back to the teacher.) Bridge.

Teacher: How about if I write "bridge" right next to it. (She does this.) I have an idea. How about if you start your story saying, "Once upon a time there was a tree with a door in it."

Charlyne: (She nods yes.) (All three children are hunched over the table watching the teacher intently as she writes. Timothy and Anthony repeat each word of this sentence slowly as the teacher writes.)

Teacher: Then what happens?

Charlyne: Then I color it in.

Teacher: (As she writes) Then—I—color—it—in. (Again, Timothy and Anthony also echo each word as the teacher writes.) Then what happens? (pause) How about if we say, "It was a magic door."

Charlyne: (Nods yes, looking very pleased.)

Teacher: What happens next?

Charlyne: (Pauses hesitantly, and then says slowly) It has colors in it.

Teacher: It—has—colors—in—it. How about if we say, "I opened the door and saw a bridge."

Charlyne:	(Nods yes.)
Teacher:	What happens next?
Charlyne:	It fell down.
Teacher:	Good! It—fell—down. Then what?
Charlyne:	It broke.
Teacher:	It—broke.
Timothy:	(Whispers in Charlyne's ear.) Say "Somebody stole the house."
Charlyne:	Somebody stole the house.
Teacher:	Somebody—stole— the house. And then. . . ?
Timothy:	(Whispers again.) Say "Somebody kidnapped the girl."
Charlyne:	(Looks at the teacher for a moment.)
Teacher:	Do you want me to write that? Do you like Timothy's ideas?
Charlyne:	(Nods yes.)
Teacher:	Then it's all right to put them in your story. Somebody— kidnapped—the—girl.
Timothy:	And the boy ate all the food.
Charlyne:	And the boy ate all the food.
Teacher:	And—the—boy—ate—all—the—food. We only have a minute left before cleanup time. Think of a good way to end your story, Charlyne.
Timothy:	The boy stole some bread.
Teacher:	Do you want that in your story?
Charlyne:	(Nods yes.)
Teacher:	The—boy—stole—some—bread. Good story!

Timothy: The end.

Teacher: The—end. Good.

The timer has sounded signaling cleanup time. The children put materials away and then gather on a rug for group time.

During group time, the teacher leads the children in acting out the three dictated stories. She reads Anthony's story to the group and asks him, "Who would you like to have help you act out this story?" He chooses Timothy. Anthony and Timothy stand in the middle of the rug as the children sit around the edge. Miss Adams reads each line of the narrative as the boys bring the words to life with the actions and voices of their characters. When it is Timothy's turn to act out his story, he reciprocates and asks Anthony to be the second character in his story.

The teacher then announces that Charlyne has written her first story. She asks Charlyne to pick children to help her act it out. The children shout and wave their hands begging for a part. The teacher asks Charlyne if she wants to play the part of the one who goes inside the magic tree. She says yes. The teacher then tells her, "You'll need someone to play the tree, someone who steals the house. . . . Charlyne, you have somebody who steals the house, and somebody who kidnaps the girl. Are they the same person or two different people?" Charlyne says they are different people, and then selects children for these parts.

The teacher again narrates as the children watch their classmates enact this magical tale. When it is over, the teacher asks the actors and actresses to sit down. Then she says, "You know, Charlyne's story had a boy stealing things from the store. Whose story does that remind you of?" The children look around; Timothy smiles, and several boys point to him. The teacher says, "Yes, it's like Timothy's story, and Timothy helped Charlyne write her first story today."

A COMMUNITY OF WRITERS AND READERS

The principle of "engaging in practice" is evident in the daily activities of Miss Adams's kindergarten classroom. These children are not "rehearsing" for real communication; rather, they are doing authentic, purposeful talking, writing, and reading. Through basic activities such as being read to, drawing, scribbling and writing, and dictating and dramatizing their own stories, the children participate in complex forms of thinking and communicating, and practice many of the basic skills necessary for writing and reading.

DICTATING AND DRAMATIZING STORIES

Because story dictation and dramatization represent one way teachers can create a community of writers and readers, we have done research on these activities in various kinds of preschool and kindergarten programs: an inner-city public school preschool, a suburban public school kindergarten, a private nursery school, and two daycare programs. (About 55 percent of the children were black, 35 percent white, and 10 percent from other racial or ethnic groups.) At each site, there was an experimental classroom where children had opportunities to dictate and dramatize stories over a twelve-week period, and a control classroom where children only dictated stories at the beginning and end of this period. At the end of the twelve weeks, dictated narratives from the two groups were compared. Narratives from the experimental group showed more complexity, richness, and coherence than did those from the control group.[6]

Dictating and dramatizing stories seemed to help children develop a better understanding of what makes a coherent story and of how to develop an idea with a beginning, a middle, and an end. In particular, acting out story ideas helps them to recognize when cause-and-effect sequences make sense to the audience, and when action sequences are undeveloped or unresolved.

In comparison with control-group children, the experimental group showed evidence of more metalinguistic and metacognitive awareness of writing and the writing process, knowledge that several researchers have identified as important for learning to read and write.[7] Children in the experimental group demonstrated their awareness of written language by making comments about letters, words, sentences, and spacing of the text on the page. Similarly, they took more initiative in the process of composing and writing down their stories. For example, they engaged others in discussion of what their story was going to be about, and they asked the researcher to reread their story to remind them of what they had written so far.

Children who participate in such activities over time learn many basic skills, some of which would be difficult to teach in a more direct and didactic way. For example, as teachers transpose children's spoken words into written symbols during dictation, children learn that writing makes words and ideas permanent, and that it produces a tangible product—words written on paper. They learn about how much time it takes to transpose an idea onto paper. Timothy and Anthony are well aware of these aspects of writing, and they show their ease and patience with the rhythm of the process as they echo Charlyne's words while the teacher writes down her story. Understanding of this aspect of the writing process may develop slowly: when children begin to dictate, they often speak too quickly and force a teacher to say "Wait, slow down. I can't write that fast." When teachers repeat each word as they write, children learn something about how words are turned into writing. Sometimes children are frustrated because writing is so much slower than the rush of their thoughts. But most children find that the rewards of dramatization make it worth disciplining their thinking to the needs of their scribe. When Anthony and Timothy begin to write stories on their own in first grade, they will already be familiar with some of the aspects of the process of translating ideas into print.

In taking dictation, Miss Adams usually writes stories in the children's own words, including some grammatical errors and dialect conventions. The purpose of the dictation is the recording of the child's ideas, and Miss Adams responds mostly to the content and meaning of what the child is saying. (This is comparable to teachers' acceptance of incorrect grammar and invented spellings in children's early writing.) How, one might ask, will children learn conventional English grammar if they are allowed to "practice" incorrect forms? Learning the conventions of written language, like learning those of oral language, is a slow and gradual process. Children learn to dictate and eventually to write with standard grammar and spelling by listening to good storybooks, talking, dictating, and writing with people who speak and write grammatically. In classrooms like Miss Adams's, children's "errors" are viewed as evidence of learning in progress rather than as mistakes that must be corrected immediately.

Anthony and Timothy are proficient storytellers, but several times during the dictation Miss Adams asks them questions such as "Do you mean 'they goed outside' or 'they went outside'?" In this way she lets the child hear

the sound of his or her own words, and also the sound
of the correct English form. Often children recognize that
the correct form reflects their intentions, and they select
it for the teacher to write. Sometimes children stick to
their own, incorrect form, and teachers like Miss Adams
respect this as what makes sense to the child at the time,
and write it down as spoken. By listening to stories, dictating stories, and acting them out, children can learn
which language forms provide the clearest expression of
their ideas. With sensitive guidance and attention to
words from their teachers, children's skill with language
(grammar, vocabulary, and expression) grows dramati-
cally through the preschool years.

Dramatization of the children's own stories, as well as
of stories from books, provides opportunities for developing story comprehension and understanding of word
meanings. Because dramatization depends solely on the
children's actions to bring words to life, it heightens children's attention to word meanings. Dramatization makes
the connection between spoken and written language direct and concrete; as a child's words are read and dramatized, children see that words must make sense.

When children first start dictating stories, their narratives often appear to be disjointed lists of characters and
events without meaningful plots. This is one of Anthony's first stories, dictated when he was 3 years old:

> Knight Rider, he can talk. Knight Rider jump. Heman
> comes and says, "I won the power of Grey Skull!" He-
> man and Knight Rider jump up in the sky. A snake
> come and bite Heman.

Gradually, as they watch and listen to their own stories,
those of their peers, and those written by adult authors
being read and acted out day after day, children develop actions and dialogue to fill out events and adven-

tures. Thus their developing understanding of narrative is shaped in the active give-and-take in the classroom every day—in play, story dictation, and the dramatization of books and stories.

Dictating a story provides opportunities for a child to learn about logical thinking and narrative structure. During dictation, teachers give children individual attention and listen carefully to their ideas. They help children to work hard at using words precisely to create a satisfying plot.

Charlyne's story exemplifies this learning process. Charlyne came to school, as many children do, not knowing what it means to make up a story and have it written down. Children create stories all day long in their play, and in conversations with peers and adults, but it is a different experience to construct a narrative that is written down and shared with others. Charlyne came into a school environment where dictation was a regular routine, and she had several weeks to observe before she answered yes to the teacher's question, "Do you want to tell a story?"

Charlyne was not the only author of her first story; it was shaped by the input of her classmates and her teacher. The questions and suggestions of Miss Adams and Timothy provided a framework for Charlyne to practice constructing a story. She began by drawing a picture, borrowing Timothy's idea of a Christmas tree and adding a door. When it was Charlyne's turn to dictate, the teacher sensed that she had trouble knowing how to make something happen in her story. The teacher tried to help her frame the elements of her story (the Christmas tree and the door) into narrative form by suggesting, "Once upon a time there was a tree with a door in it." When Charlyne continued to treat her story more as a drawing than as a narrative (by having the next line be about coloring in the door), the teacher again showed her narrative possibilities by suggesting that the door could be a "magic door." Again Charlyne responded as if describing a drawing: "It has colors in it." Miss Adams then tried to show Charlyne how to make a plot unfold, by suggesting that she open the door in the tree; the teacher offered help by building on Charlyne's own ideas.

Timothy and Anthony also helped Charlyne, demonstrating a community of writers and readers in action. Charlyne needed to learn how to pose a problem and then resolve it. Timothy in effect asked her to use an idea he had been thinking about, and she was delighted to do so. Timothy then showed her how he would play out that idea as he prompted her with additional ideas. In this learning process, Charlyne was not defeated by her lack of understanding of the activity. Instead, she was able to become an author alongside her more competent peers by participating in an activity with others who adapted to her level of need, and who encouraged her to contribute as much as she could.

THE TEACHER'S ROLE

Without the teacher, the dictation and dramatization of stories could not take place. The teacher first of all provides opportunities for children to compose stories by making these activities available during the school day. As can be seen during the dictation of Charlyne's story, the teacher's role includes being a scribe, a friendly editor, and an interested reader and audience for children's ideas. Her questions and comments help children develop more complete narratives than they could achieve by themselves. The teacher demonstrates respect for children's ideas, interest in knowing what they are thinking about, and willingness to help extend and clarify their thinking by asking questions and talking with them about their story ideas.

During the dramatization of stories, the teacher's role is that of stage manager and narrator. The teacher's vision of how ideas can be enacted and brought to life shapes the children's possibilities for learning. As stage manager, the teacher helps create a space for the story characters, and then encourages the children to act out their roles and speak their lines according to the script. Her narration forms the thread that holds the characters and the unfolding drama together.

When Miss Adams led the dramatization of Charlyne's story, she began by reading, "Once upon a time, there was a tree with a door in it." She then said to Charlyne, the leading character, "Show us the tree that you find that has a door in it." Charlyne used her arms and hands to make the outline of a tree in the air. Miss Adams then added, "Show us where the door is." Charlyne made a door shape with her finger that would place it inside the tree she had just traced in the air. Miss Adams said "Good!" and continued with the narration, "Then I color it in." She coached Charlyne, "Show us how you color it," and Charlyne pretended to pick up a crayon and made large sweeping coloring motions in the air.

In both dictation and dramatization, the teacher's questions and comments can challenge children to express themselves and to portray the meaning of their stories as fully as possible. Teachers can also help children make connections between their stories and other events in the classroom, connections that create a stronger sense of community.

DRAMATIZATION

When children begin to dictate, their stories are often descriptions of events from their daily lives—perhaps telling about an outing with family members or what they saw on TV recently, or retelling a story that has been read to them, such as *The Three Bears*. As stories are acted out, the narratives that children dictate begin to change. The stories seem to develop a social purpose; that is, they reflect a kind of dialogue with others in the group. Some stories contain themes borrowed from peers or from the books being read to the group; these themes are transformed in various ways by different children. Stories may be written to celebrate a friendship or to resolve tensions between friends; stories reflect children's worries and fears and, sometimes, how to manage them. Stories celebrate special events such as a birthday or Valentine's Day; and some stories explore ideas that have been raised in dramatic play. The dictation and dramatization of stories help teachers to develop an active community of writers and readers in their classrooms as children become intimately involved in using written language to communicate with one another, and to make connections with the ideas and thinking of those around them.

In our research, boys in the experimental classrooms dictated as many stories as did girls—slightly more in some classrooms. This was not true for the control classrooms, where girls tended to dictate more stories than boys. This finding is noteworthy given previous research that points to generally earlier language and literacy development for girls than for boys,[8] and the fact that boys far outnumber girls as reading failures in school. Our results confirm Paley's observation that boys want to participate in the dictation of stories when dramatization is included. As one kindergarten boy remarked, "It's not a story if you don't act it out."

Our research also suggests that the dictation and dramatization of stories can strengthen writing and reading skills for children with oral and written language disorders.[9] Learning disabled children ages 6 to 14 who participated in story dictation and dramatization activities (either in public school classrooms or in a remediation clinic) showed the same patterns of growth over a twelve-week period as the children in the experimental groups in the study we have described. Most important, knowing their stories would be dramatized motivated learning disabled children to dictate and eventually to write their own narratives, so that their reading and writing skills improved as they participated as authors, actors, audience, and literary critics in their classroom community.

Our description of Miss Adams's kindergarten classroom provides a glimpse of the interrelationships of fantasy play, conversation, dictation, and dramatization of children's stories in the course of an afternoon. Story ideas come to children as they participate in an environment where, in Eleanor Duckworth's phrase, "the having of wonderful ideas" is valued and encouraged. Dramatization of stories fulfills many of the needs served by dramatic play, with the added advantage of increased control over who will play each role and how the scenario will unfold. The chance to share ideas with others, to hear what other children are thinking, and to develop familiar themes in new ways is so rewarding that it brings children to story dictation day after day to write for, with, and in response to the writings of other community members.

BRIDGES TO SCHOOL

Preschool and kindergarten programs teach children a great deal about literacy, but in ways that do not look much like traditional elementary school instruction.

What teachers in early childhood programs accomplish, when they incorporate books, paper, and pencils into their classrooms in some of the ways described here, is to create a community setting that embodies many of the values and practices of a school-oriented literate culture, and that gives children opportunities to participate in this literate culture in a way appropriate to their level of development.

In preschool and kindergarten classrooms built around basic literacy activities, words—both spoken and written—and their meanings matter first and foremost. Words become the main cultural tool that binds community members together. Curricula built around play, stories, and the dialogues that take place among community members provide children not only with individual attention from teachers but also with the vast enrichment of ideas that comes from daily contact with their peers. When having good ideas, learning to think clearly, and expressing ideas in writing and in conversation are shared pursuits and reasons for being together, children learn what it can mean to be literate, and thus are likely to develop the motivation to become literate themselves.

Preschool and kindergarten programs based on these ideas are likely to benefit children from a range of home environments. For some, basic activities will extend the kinds of learning and development that have been taking place at home. For others, such activities can help build bridges between home and school, between familiar activities and unfamiliar ones. This is what was happening for Charlyne in Miss Adams's classroom. Children like Charlyne can learn literacy skills in classroom environments that allow them to build on the resources that every child brings to this setting—the capacity to play and the capacity to talk with others.

There are many debates in the field of education over how to meet the challenge of educating children from various cultural backgrounds, particularly inner-city minority children. Regardless of children's home experiences with writing and reading, we believe that it is the schools' responsibility to provide classrooms and curricula that involve children in talking, playing, writing, reading, and listening to one another and their teachers. Classrooms built around play, open-ended conversations, and basic literacy activities can help children, whatever their backgrounds, feel at an early age that they want to come to school, that they want to learn to read and write—and that they will be able to do so.

Building bridges between diverse home experiences and the demands of formal schooling is not easy. It requires respect for the subtle and complex role of the teacher as the organizer and leader of the classroom community, and for the capacity of young children to use symbols. Children's ability to use and develop symbols is most likely to flourish when they can take an active role in the classroom, and when they can have some measure of control over their own participation in a community of writers and readers. Encouraging children to use the full range of their linguistic, cognitive, social, and symbolic resources for learning is the best way to help every child become a competent member of the larger community of writers and readers.

The approach of one Trackton teacher when greeting a class of first graders is one that more teachers might find useful:

> At the beginning of the year, I tell my students: "Reading and writing are things you do all the time—at home, on the bus, riding your bike, at the barber shop. You can read, and you do every day before you ever come to school. You can also play baseball. Reading and writing

are like baseball or football. You play baseball and football at home, at the park, wherever you want to, but when you come to school or go to a summer program at the Neighborhood Center, you get help on techniques, the gloves to buy, the way to throw, and the way to slide. School does that for reading and writing. We all read and write a lot of the time, lots of places. School isn't much different except here we work on techniques, and we practice a lot—under a coach. I'm the coach."[10]

7 / Conclusion

As we have seen, learning to write and read begins early and involves both young children and the significant people in their lives. Becoming literate is not just a matter of learning a set of technical skills (decoding, handwriting, spelling) that are typically taught in elementary school. Rather, literacy consists of particular ways of making, interpreting, and communicating meaning with written language, and becoming literate requires mastering a complex set of understandings, attitudes, expectations, and behaviors, as well as specific skills, related to written language.

Many young children engage in a range of activities related to writing and reading well before they encounter formal literacy instruction in school. Some of these may look quite different from more mature forms of these pursuits, as for example, 2-year-old Jennifer's "reading" a story about a bear from a "book" made of two leaves, or 4-year-old Joshua's writing a poem that includes dots representing "bullets making gun noises." Literacy development often begins in children's early symbol-using activities: in play and fantasy, in scribbling and drawing, and in pretend reading and writing. Play is where much of young children's exploration and learning takes place. When books, paper, and writing materials are among the objects children play with, important literacy learning can occur. Children can use their experience with talking, drawing, and playing to build bridges to writing and reading. Through play, children can acquire a range of information and skills related to writing and reading, as well as feelings and expectations about themselves as potential writers and readers. This multifaceted body of knowledge and attitudes constitutes "early" or "emergent" literacy.

Literacy enters young children's lives in a variety of ways. Early experiences with literacy may be initiated by the child or by other people, they may be playful or work-like, and they may take place at home, in the neighborhood, or in a preschool or daycare program. They include pretending to write and read fairy tales and poems, writing a thank-you letter to a distant grandmother, receiving instruction in how to form the letters of the word DANGER or how to spell one's name, listening to a story being read aloud, or reading passages from the Bible. The range and diversity of early literacy experiences suggests that there are many ways that children make connections with writing and reading, and many pathways into literacy.

Early literacy development does not simply happen; rather, it is a social process, embedded in children's relationships with parents, siblings, grandparents, friends, caretakers, and teachers. In *Gnys at Wrk*, Glenda Bissex described the "drama" of one child's developing mastery of written language. The "genius" in her story is the mind of the individual child at work, seeking, and at times struggling hard, to learn to write and read. We have tried to present another essential part of early literacy development: the social fabric of young children's lives.

Early experiences with literacy are embedded in the

relationships, activities, and settings of children's everyday lives. It is people who make writing and reading interesting and meaningful to young children. Family members, caretakers, and teachers play critical roles in early literacy development by serving as models, providing materials, demonstrating their use, reading to children, offering help, instruction, and encouragement, and communicating hopes and expectations. To their interactions with young children, these people bring their attitudes and expectations, both conscious and unconscious, about writing and reading, and about the child's eventual development as a writer and reader. The "literacy lessons" they provide for young children may be embedded in playful responses to pretend writing and reading or may consist of more direct, didactic instruction in letter formation, spelling, and decoding.

To these relationships and activities, children bring their curiosity, their interest in communicating and interacting with others, and their inclination to be a part of family and community life. They also bring their desire to use and control materials and tools that they perceive as important to the people around them—their urge to "do it myself." And they bring their willingness to seek help from more proficient writers and readers. Interacting with more competent writers and readers, children serve as "spontaneous apprentices" (in George Miller's phrase) as they learn about written language and how to use it for various purposes.

It is both what children *and* what other people bring to these interactions that shapes what children learn and how they come to see the eventual place of literacy in their own lives. Young children stand the best chance of developing a good foundation for writing and reading if their learning about literacy is anchored in their relationships with caretakers, peers, and other community members, and if it is tied to contexts and activities that have personal meaning and value for them.

What is the relationship between early experiences with literacy and later, long-term literacy development? There are as yet no definitive answers to this question, but as in other aspects of psychological development, we assume that there *is* a relationship between early literacy experience and later mature literacy. How this relationship unfolds for a particular child will depend on several factors which interact with one another in complex ways. These include the child's interests, temperament, and personality, as well as the nature and quality of the instruction the child encounters in school.

Learning is also affected by the continuity—or lack of continuity—between the child's experiences with literacy at home and those encountered in school. Some children have a difficult time making connections between home and school experiences with writing and reading. As we have seen, most children know something about writing and reading by the time they start school. The hard work for teachers, as Courtney Cazden and Shirley Brice Heath in particular have demonstrated, comes in discovering what children already know about writing and reading and then helping them make connections with what the school wants them to know.[1]

How literacy ultimately develops will depend on whether writing and reading become meaningful parts of the child's life. This, in turn, will depend on people who are important to the child—both inside and outside of school—and on the messages they communicate about the child's development as a writer and reader.

Notes
Suggested Reading
Index

Notes

1 / WHAT IS LITERACY?

1. F. Erickson, "School Literacy, Reasoning and Civility: An Anthropologist's Perspective," *Review of Educational Research* 54, no. 4 (Winter 1984): 525.
2. S. B. Heath, "What No Bedtime Story Means: Narrative Skills at Home and at School," *Language in Society* 11, no. 2 (1982): 49–76.
3. J. Cook-Gumperz, "Introduction," in J. Cook-Gumperz, ed., *The Social Construction of Literacy* (Cambridge: Cambridge University Press, 1986), pp. 1–15.
4. See D. M. Smith, "The Anthropology of Literacy Acquisition," in B. B. Schieffelin, ed., *The Acquisition of Literacy: Ethnographic Perspectives* (Norwood, N.J.: Ablex, 1986), pp. 261–275.
5. D. Holdaway, *The Foundations of Literacy* (Sydney, Australia: Ashton Scholastic, 1979); W. H. Teale and E. Sulzby, *Emergent Literacy: Writing and Reading* (Norwood, N.J.: Ablex, 1986).
6. R. Gundlach, M. Farr, and J. Cook-Gumperz, "Writing and Reading in the Community," in A. H. Dyson, ed., *Collaboration through Writing and Reading: Exploring Possibilities* (Urbana, Ill.: National Council of Teachers of English, 1989), pp. 93–94.

2 / BRIDGES TO LITERACY

1. L. S. Vygotsky, *Mind in Society* (Cambridge, Mass.: Harvard University Press, 1978). A. H. Dyson, "Transitions and Tensions: Interrelationships between the Drawing,

Talking, and Dictating of Young Children," *Research in the Teaching of English* 20, no. 4 (December 1986): 279–409, p. 407. R. Gundlach, "Children as Writers: The Beginnings of Learning to Write," in M. Nystrand, ed., *What Writers Know* (New York: Academic Press, 1982), pp. 129–147.

2. H. Gardner and D. Wolf, "Editors' Notes: Dimensions of Early Symbol Use," in H. Gardner and D. Wolf, eds., *Early Symbolization* (San Francisco: Jossey-Bass, 1979), p. vii.

3. Gundlach, "Children as Writers"; Dyson, "Transitions and Tensions."

4. H. Gardner, D. Wolf, and A. Smith. "Max and Molly: Individual Differences in Early Artistic Symbolization," in H. Gardner, ed., *Art, Mind and Brain: A Cognitive Approach to Creativity* (New York: Basic Books, 1982), pp. 110–127, p. 112.

5. J. Bruner, "Introduction," in B. Tizard and D. Harvey, *Biology of Play* (London: Heinemann Medical Books, 1977), p. v. C. Garvey, *Play* (Cambridge, Mass.: Harvard University Press, 1977).

6. H. Gardner, "The Birth of Literary Imagination," in Gardner, ed., *Art, Mind and Brain*, pp. 168–183, p. 170.

7. J. Britton, "Writing and the Story World," in B. M. Kroll and G. Wells, eds., *Explorations in the Development of Writing* (New York: John Wiley, 1983); J. Bruner, "Language, Mind, and Reading," in H. Goelman, A. Oberg, and F. Smith, eds., *Awakening to Literacy* (Exeter, N.H.: Heinemann, 1984), pp. 193–200. L. Galda, "Narrative Competence: Play, Storytelling, and Story Comprehension," in A. Pellegrini and T. Yawkey, eds., *The Development of Oral and Written Language in Social Contexts* (Norwood, N.J.: Ablex, 1984).

8. C. Garvey, "Some Properties of Social Play," *Merrill Palmer Quarterly*, 20 (1974): 163–180. C. Garvey and R. Berndt, "The Organization of Pretend Play" (paper presented at the Annual Meeting of the American Psychological Association, Chicago, September 1975), p. 9.

9. G. G. Fein, "Play and the Acquisition of Symbols," *Cur-

rent Topics in Early Childhood Education 11 (1979): 195–225, p. 206.

10. J. Bruner, "Nature and Uses of Immaturity," in J. Bruner, A. Jolly, and K. Sylva, eds., *Play: Its Role in Development and Evolution* (New York: Basic Books, 1976), pp. 28–64; B. Sutton-Smith, "Epilogue: Play as Performance," in B. Sutton-Smith, ed., *Play and Learning* (New York: Gardner Press, 1979), pp. 295–322.

3 / WRITING

1. Gundlach, "Children as Writers."
2. D. Taylor, *Family Literacy: Young Children Learning to Read and Write* (Exeter, N.H.: Heinemann, 1983). G. Bissex, *Gnys at Wrk* (Cambridge, Mass.: Harvard University Press, 1980), p. 23.
3. Bruner, "Language, Mind, and Reading," p. 196.
4. C. Cazden, "Play with Language and Metalinguistic Awareness," in Bruner, Jolly, and Sylvia, eds., *Play: Its Role in Development and Evolution*, pp. 603–608.
5. A. H. Dyson, "The Emergence of Visible Language: Interrelationships between Drawing and Early Writing, *Visible Language* 16, no. 4 (Autumn 1982). Dyson, "Transitions and Tensions." Gundlach, "Children as Writers."
6. Taylor, *Family Literacy*, p. 37.
7. Gundlach, "Children as Writers," p. 143.
8. F. M. Stott, "Making Meaning Together: Motivation for Learning to Write," in K. Field, B. Cohler, and G. Wool, eds., *Motive and Meaning: Psychoanalytic Perspectives on Learning and Education* (New York: International Universities Press, in press).
9. J. B. McLane and D. Graziano, "Writing in an After-School Program," manuscript, Erikson Institute, 1987; and see McLane, "Writing as a Social Process," in L. Moll, ed., *Vygotskian Perspectives on Education* (Cambridge: Cambridge University Press, in press).
10. Holdaway, *Foundations of Literacy*, p. 36.
11. M. Clay, *What Did I Write?* (Portsmouth, N.H.: Heine-

mann, 1975); A. H. Dyson, "Individual Differences in Emerging Writing," in M. Farr, ed., *Children's Early Writing Development* (Norwood, N.J.: Ablex, 1985); E. Sulzby, "Writing and Reading: Signs of Oral and Written Language Organization in the Young Child," in Teale and Sulzby, eds., *Emergent Literacy*, pp. 50–89; Gundlach, "Children as Writers."

12. H. Gardner, *Artful Scribbles: The Significance of Children's Drawings* (New York: Basic Books, 1980).

13. M. Baghban, *Our Daughter Learns to Read and Write: A Case Study from Birth to Three* (Newark, Del.: International Reading Association, 1984), p. 48.

14. Clay, *What Did I Write?*

15. E. Ferreiro, "The Interplay between Information and Assimilation in Beginning Literacy," in Teale and Sulzby, eds., *Emergent Literacy*, pp. 15–49, p. 31.

16. J. Harste, V. Woodward, and C. Burke, *Language Stories and Literacy Lessons* (Portsmouth, N.H.: Heinemann, 1984).

17. Bissex, *Gnys at Wrk;* C. A. Temple, R. G. Nathan, and N. A. Burris, *The Beginnings of Writing* (Boston: Allyn and Bacon, 1982).

18. Temple, Nathan, and Burris, *Beginnings of Writing*, p. 78.

19. C. Chomsky, "Write Now, Read Later," in C. B. Cazden, ed., *Language in Early Childhood Education* (Washington, D.C.: National Association for the Education of Young Children, 1981), pp. 141–149, p. 149.

20. Clay, *What Did I Write?;* Temple, Nathan, and Burris, *Beginnings of Writing;* Ferreiro, "The Interplay between Information and Assimilation."

21. A. H. Dyson, "Talking with Young Children Writing," *Childhood Education*, September-October 1982, p. 31.

22. Clay, *What Did I Write?*, p. 46. Temple, Nathan, and Burris, *Beginnings of Writing*, p. 47.

23. Bruner, "Language, Mind, and Reading," p. 196.

24. L. S. Flower and J. R. Hayes, "The Dynamics of Composing: Making Plans and Juggling Constraints," in L. W. Gregg and E. R. Steinberg, eds., *Cognitive Processes in Writing* (Hillsdale, N.J.: Erlbaum, 1980), pp. 31–50, p. 33.

M. Scardamalia, "How Children Cope with the Cognitive Demands of Writing," in C. H. Frederiksen and J. F. Dominic, eds., *Writing: Process, Development and Communication* (Hillsdale, N.J.: Erlbaum, 1981), pp. 81–103, p. 81. P. Elbow, *Writing about Teachers* (London: Oxford University Press, 1973), p. 135.

25. D. H. Graves, *Writing: Teachers and Children at Work* (Exeter, N.H.: Heinemann, 1983); A. H. Dyson, "Research Currents: The Emergence of Children's Written Voices," *Language Arts* 64, no. 6 (October 1987): 654.
26. D. H. Graves, "Let Children Show Us How to Help Them Write," *Visible Language* 13 (1979): 16–28, p. 19.
27. Dyson, "Research Currents," pp. 651, 652.
28. Dyson, "Research Currents," p. 654. Graves, *Writing*, pp. 252, 227.
29. C. Bereiter and M. Scardamalia, "From Conversation to Composition: The Role of Instruction in a Developmental Process," in R. Glaser, ed., *Advances in Instructional Psychology*, vol. 2 (Hillsdale, N.J.: Erlbaum, 1982), p. 36.
30. Graves, *Writing*, p. 235. R. Gundlach, "On the Nature and Development of Children's Writing," in Frederiksen and Dominic, eds., *Writing: Process, Development and Communication*, pp. 133–151.
31. Graves, *Writing*; L. Calkins, *The Art of Teaching Writing* (Portsmouth, N.H.: Heinemann, 1986).
32. Dyson, "Research Currents," p. 657.

4 / READING

1. R. C. Anderson, E. Hiebert, J. A. Scott, and I. A. G. Wilkinson, *Becoming a Nation of Readers: The Report of the Commission on Reading* (Washington, D.C.: National Academy of Education, 1985), p. 7.
2. Bissex, *Gnys at Wrk*, p. 119.
3. S. Kontos, "What Preschool Children Know about Reading and How They Learn It," *Young Children*, November 1986, pp. 58–66, p. 58.
4. M. V. Zintz, *The Reading Process* (Dubuque, Ia.: William C.

Brown, 1970). W. Gray, *On Their Own in Reading* (Chicago: Scott Foresman, 1948), pp. 35–37 (as discussed in Zintz, p. 5).

5. S. B. Heath, "The Functions and Uses of Literacy" in S. deCastell, A. Luke, and K. Egan, eds., *Literacy, Society and Schooling* (Cambridge: Cambridge University Press, 1986), p. 20.

6. S. B. Heath, *Ways with Words* (Cambridge: Cambridge University Press, 1983); Heath, "The Functions and Uses of Literacy."

7. C. Snow and A. Ninio, "The Contracts of Literacy: What Children Learn from Learning to Read Books," in Teale and Sulzby, eds., *Emergent Literacy*, p. 121.

8. H. Werner and B. Kaplan, *Symbol Formation* (New York: Wiley, 1963) (as discussed in Snow and Ninio, p. 122).

9. A. Ninio and J. Bruner, "The Achievement and Antecedents of Labeling," *Journal of Child Language* 5 (1978): 1–15.

10. J. Bruner, "Learning the Mother Tongue," *Human Nature*, September 1978, pp. 43–49, p. 45. J. S. DeLoache, "What's This? Maternal Questions in Joint Picture Book Reading with Toddlers," *Quarterly Newsletter of the Laboratory of Comparative Human Cognition* 6, no. 4 (October 1984): 87–94, p. 90.

11. J. W. Lindfors, "The Interaction of Language and Literature: A Case of Mother-Child Dialogue" (paper presented at the 16th International Congress of the International Federation for Modern Languages and Literatures, Budapest, 1984), p. 8.

12. DeLoache, "What's This?" p. 91. W. H. Teale, "Reading to Young Children: Its Significance for Literacy Development," in Goelman, Oberg, and Smith, eds., *Awakening to Literacy*, p. 117.

13. W. H. Teale, "Toward a Theory of How Children Learn to Read and Write Naturally" *Language Arts* 59, no. 6 (September 1982): 555–570, p. 561.

14. Baghban, *Our Daughter Learns to Read and Write*, p. 101.

15. R. Scollon and S. B. K. Scollon, *Narrative, Literacy and Face in Interethnic Communication* (Norwood, N.J.: Ablex, 1981);

Holdaway, *Foundations of Literacy;* Teale and Sulzby, *Emergent Literacy.*

16. J. Bruner, "Reading for Signs of Life," *New York Review of Books,* April 1, 1982.
17. D. Feitelson, B. Kita, and Z. Goldstein, "Effects of Reading Series-Stories to First Graders on Their Comprehension and Use of Language" (Haifa, Israel: School of Education, Haifa University, 1986), as discussed in J. M. Mason, and J. Allen, *A Review of Emergent Literacy with Implications for Research and Practice in Reading,* Technical Report no. 379 (Champaign, Ill.: Center For The Study of Reading, 1986), p. 57.
18. J. C. Oates, "The Making of a Writer" *New York Times Book Review,* July 11, 1982, p. 1.
19. Holdaway, *Foundations of Literacy,* p. 44.
20. E. Sulzby, "Children's Emergent Reading of Favorite Storybooks: A Developmental Study," *Reading Research Quarterly,* Summer 1985, pp. 458–481.
21. E. Ferreiro and A. Teberosky, *Literacy before Schooling* (Portsmouth, N.H.: Heinemann Educational Books, 1979).
22. Temple, Nathan, and Burris, *Beginnings of Writing.*
23. D. Tedeschi, "The Emerging Reading and Writing of a 5½-Year-Old Boy," manuscript, Erikson Institute, July 1988.
24. Bruner, "Reading for Signs of Life"; J. Chall, *Learning to Read: The Great Debate* (New York: McGraw-Hill, 1967).
25. M. Cole and P. Griffin, "A Socio-Historical Approach to Remediation," in deCastell, Luke, and Egan, eds., *Literacy, Society and Schooling.*

5 / AT HOME AND IN THE NEIGHBORHOOD

1. H. J. Leichter, "Families as Environments for Literacy," in Goelman, Oberg, and Smith, *Awakening to Literacy,* pp. 38–50, p. 40.
2. B. B. Schieffelin and M. Cochran-Smith, "Learning to Read Culturally: Literacy Before Schooling," in Goelman, Oberg, and Smith, *Awakening to Literacy,* pp. 3–23. McLane, "Working with Head Start Parents."

3. Gundlach, Farr, and Cook-Gumperz, "Writing and Reading in the Community."

4. R. Gundlach, J. B. McLane, F. M. Stott, and G. D. Mc-Namee, "The Social Foundations of Children's Early Writing Development," in M. Farr, ed., *Children's Early Writing Development* (Norwood, N.J.: Ablex, 1985); Heath, "What No Bedtime Story Means"; Heath, *Ways with Words*"; Schieffelin and Cochran-Smith, "Learning to Read Culturally"; Scollon and Scollon, *Narrative, Literacy, and Face*; D. Taylor and C. Dorsey-Gaines, *Growing Up Literate: Learning from Inner-City Families* (Portsmouth, N.H.: Heinemann, 1988); McLane, "Working with Head Start Parents."

5. J. Bruner, *Child's Talk: Learning to Use Language* (New York: W. W. Norton, 1983); J. Bruner, "The Ontogenesis of Speech Arts," *Journal of Child Language* 2 (1975): 1–19.

6. Stott, "Making Meaning Together"; Gundlach, McLane, Stott, and McNamee, "The Social Foundations of Children's Early Writing Development."

7. See L. D. Delpit, "Skills and Other Dilemmas of a Progressive Black Educator," *Harvard Educational Review* 56, no. 4 (November 1986): 379–385.

8. Schieffelin and Cochran-Smith, "Learning to Read Culturally," p. 21.

9. These parents may also have given their children instruction at home in the kinds of "work habits and skills" that Lily Wong Fillmore observed being taught in Chinese immigrant families from Hong Kong and Vietnam. Parents in these families gave their preschool children many tasks that helped them develop "the skills and abilities needed" for schoolwork such as "workbook exercises, . . . ditto-sheets, and the like." L. W. Fillmore, "Now or Later? Issues Related to the Early Education of Minority Group Children" (paper presented at the Council of Chief State School Officers, Summer Meetings, Boston, August 2, 1988).

10. Schieffelin and Cochran-Smith, "Learning to Read Culturally," pp. 19–20.

6 / IN PRESCHOOL AND KINDERGARTEN

1. R. Gundlach, "The Place of Computers in the Teaching of Writing" in A. M. Lesgold and F. Reif, eds., *Computers in Education: Realizing the Potential* (Washington, D.C.: U.S. Department of Education, 1983).
2. J. Lindfors, *Children's Language and Learning* (Englewood Cliffs, N.J.: Prentice Hall, 1987), p. 253.
3. Lindfors, *Children's Language and Learning*, p. 254.
4. Cole and Griffin, "A Socio-Historical Approach to Remediation."
5. V. G. Paley, *Wally's Stories* (Cambridge, Mass.: Harvard University Press, 1981), pp. 11–12.
6. G. D. McNamee, J. McLane, P. M. Cooper, and S. M. Kerwin, "Cognition and Affect in Early Literacy Development," *Early Childhood Development and Care* 20 (1985): 229–244.
7. C. Cazden, *Language in Early Childhood Education* (Washington, D.C.: National Association for the Education of Young Children, 1981); Holdaway, *Foundations of Literacy;* M. Clay, *Reading: The Patterning of Complex Behavior* (Portsmouth, N.H.: Heinemann Educational Books, 1980); M. Donaldson, *Children's Minds* (New York: W. W. Norton, 1978).
8. J. S. Chall, "Reading Ability in Boys and Girls," *Harvard Educational Review* 53, no. 4 (November 1983): 439–443.
9. G. D. McNamee and G. Harris-Schmidt, "Narration and Dramatization with Learning Disabled Children" *Quarterly Newsletter of The Laboratory of Comparative Human Cognition* 7, no. 1 (January 1985): 6–15; G. Harris-Schmidt and G. D. McNamee, "Children as Authors and Actors: Literacy Development through Basic Activities," *Child Language, Teaching and Therapy* 2, no. 1 (1986): 63–73.
10. Heath, *Ways with Words*, p. 289.

7 / CONCLUSION

1. C. Cazden, *Classroom Discourse: The Language of Teaching and Learning* (Portsmouth, N.H.: Heinemann, 1988); Heath, *Ways with Words.*

Suggested Reading

R. C. Anderson, E. Hiebert, J. A. Scott, and I. A. G. Wilkinson. *Becoming a Nation of Readers: The Report of the Commission on Reading*. Washington, D.C.: National Academy of Education, 1985.

G. Bissex. *Gnys at Wrk*. Cambridge, Mass.: Harvard University Press, 1980.

A. H. Dyson. *Multiple Worlds of Child Writers: Friends Learning to Write*. New York: Teachers College Press, 1989.

D. Holdaway. *The Foundations of Literacy*. Sydney, Australia: Ashton Scholastic, 1979.

V. G. Paley. *Wally's Stories*. Cambridge, Mass.: Harvard University Press, 1981.

W. H. Teale and E. Sulzby, eds. *Emergent Literacy: Writing and Reading*. Norwood, N.J.: Ablex, 1986.

C. A. Temple, R. G. Nathan, and N. A. Burris. *The Beginnings of Writing*. Boston: Allyn and Bacon, 1982.

Index